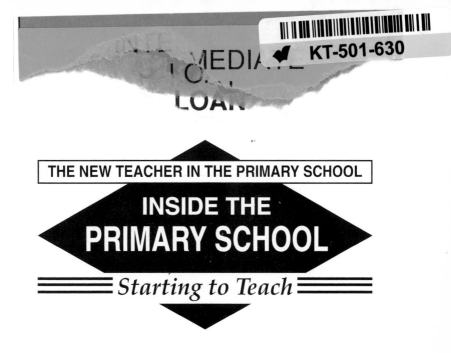

THE NEW TEACHER IN THE PRIMARY SCHOOL

INSIDE THE PRIMARY SCHOOL
Starting to Teach

DENIS HAYES

Series Editor: Professor Michael Newby

Series Editor: Professor Michael Newby

First published 1993 by Southgate Publishers Ltd

Southgate Publishers Ltd
Glebe House, Church Street, Crediton, Devon EX17 2AF

Printed and bound in Great Britain by Short Run Press, Exeter, Devon.

British Library Cataloguing in Publication Data.
A CIP catalogue record for this book is available from the British Library.

ISBN 1–85741–066–1

*This book is dedicated to my father
and to the memory of
my aunt, Florence Newton.*

PREFACE

Primary teachers have a formidable responsibility. In each year of their professional lives, they play a significant part in the daily experience and future development of twenty-five or more children. Many hundreds of adults will live their lives in ways influenced by the skill, hard work and commitment of a single primary teacher, years before. Of course, the teacher is not the only influence on a child: parents and the wider family, the rest of the school, and the social, political, economic and spiritual environment are important factors too. But at the heart of the educational process it is the teacher who most directly affects the pace and quality of the child's growth.

Each stage of children's education is significant, from their first day at school to the day they leave for work or college. None the less, the first period of formal education, the years from five to eleven, is vital *in particular ways*. The primary teacher's work is partly to help children discover what is there inside and to nurture it, and partly to enrich children's development by introducing them progressively to the richness of the world outside. All primary teachers aim to help their pupils become more skilful, more knowledgeable, more understanding, more confident – emotionally and physically. If they are good at their work, they never stop learning to do these things better tomorrow than they did today.

The New Teacher and the Primary School is a series of books written by successful educators who are committed to sharing their considerable experience with those preparing to teach and with qualified but relatively inexperienced professionals.

Teaching is a complex undertaking, but the writers' aims have been to offer straightforward, well-informed advice, and to challenge the reader to make sense of his or her growing experience of teaching in the light of what they have written. Each book in the series is intended to help new teachers become more able to meet the needs of those they teach.

Indirectly, therefore, the series is dedicated to each child who goes to school during that first, crucial decade of life. Directly, it is for teachers, now and in the future.

Professor Michael Newby
University of Plymouth

CONTENTS

INTRODUCTION

This book was written to help student teachers succeed in their teaching practice in the primary school. It explores the practice from the time you first learn about your placement in school, through your preliminary visits and early planning and lesson preparation, to the time when you take responsibility for individual children, small groups and the whole class. Whether you are about to begin your first or final practice, this book is for you.

You may have recently left school, or be returning to study after a gap of some years, studying for the BEd degree. Alternatively, you may already have completed your first degree and be busy spending a single year completing a postgraduate certificate (the PGCE). You may even be one of the few people working for the PGCE through the Articled Teachers' scheme, spending most of your time in school over two years, supported by professional staff from school and college. Whatever your route into teaching, teaching practice will form a crucial part of the process. Indeed, without succeeding here, you will never qualify as a teacher. This book is intended to help you gain that qualification.

You have already made a significant choice in deciding to teach in the primary school, for the primary school is where the foundations are laid for the rest of a person's life. Despite the many changes to the educational system over recent years, many things stay the same: the need for children to learn; the relationship between teacher and pupil; the concerns of parents; the variety of feeling and experience in the community of the primary school. The teacher's task goes beyond the common understanding of 'teachers teaching and children learning'. It involves an understanding of the needs of children and their families and a belief that life can be better if adult and pupil can discover together the excitement of working and co-operating in search of a shared goal. This sense of common purpose is what makes teaching much more than just another job.

Chapter 1 leads up to the first, all-important day of your practice in a new school.

Chapter 2 is about the class teacher and the way she organises her class, her materials, the children and the activities they engage in.

Chapter 3 is about the children and includes case studies to help you.

Advice about long- and short-term planning is offered in **Chapter 4**, including links with the National Curriculum, keeping a school-practice file, preparing individual lesson plans, evaluating your performance, and keeping records.

Chapter 5 sets out the range of alternatives facing you during teaching practice and shows how to establish your priorities.

Chapter 6 guides you in reflecting upon your current practice and looking ahead to ways in which you might build upon it.

The central idea in this book is that good primary teaching balances practical skill with thoughtful and reflective analysis. If you can achieve this balance during your time in school, you will have taken an important step towards realising your ambition of becoming a professional teacher.

1

FROM COLLEGE TO SCHOOL

Whether you are on a BEd or PGCE course, you will spend some of your time in college and some in school. You are going to have to find the rhythm as you move between these two places. The balance and pattern of this time will vary, but all teacher education courses try to complement one with the other. The college-based components will support the work in school and help to make your teaching experience more effective; the school-based element should show you in practice what you have read, written, spoken and thought about in college.

School experience takes a variety of forms, including spending one day with a group of other students in a school, to an extended period in a classroom working with the class teacher during teaching practice. This practice may last from a few weeks in the early stages of a course to as much as a complete term by the end. You will do practices in more than one school to gain a variety and a depth of experience.

Before you begin your teaching practice you will have the chance to spend a few days in the school on a preliminary visit. This is an important time, when you go into the classroom to meet the class teacher and children with whom you'll be working. You will return to the college with a clearer picture of what the school expects from you, including information about the children, a provisional timetable, and an idea about the class teacher's teaching approach. You will come back to the college to plan your lessons and consult with tutors before the proper practice starts. Articled teachers face a slightly different procedure, but the principles of liaison are essentially the same.

Your practice school

You scan the pages on the noticeboard notifying students of their school placement. Here is yours: 'Gritpark Street Primary, Smugglers Way; Headteacher: Mrs. I. Smackalot.' Your friend is placed in 'Buttercup Meadow Infant School; Headteacher: Miss V. R. Gentle.' Looks as if luck has deserted you.

But what is it really like? Don't make too many assumptions. Other students may have been placed in the same school on another occasion, so ask for their impressions, but realise that they may be quite different from the ones you will form. More important than other people's recollections will be your own first impressions on your preliminary visit. These will not only allow you to discover something about the school, but allow those in the school to learn something about you.

Schools and student teachers

Schools are not required to take students, but most do because they realise how important it is that the next generation of teachers are well prepared in the real world of schools and classrooms. That said, it usually means more, rather than less, work for schools when students arrive, and for this reason teachers hope that their student will be someone who is willing to contribute to the life of the school. They are not so impressed with students who claim to know everything before they begin, or students who wait passively to be told exactly what to do and who cannot take the initiative for themselves. Schools do not like students who disrupt their routine too much, or cause too many changes, or make life more difficult for them than it already is. They do want students who will be open, pleasant and hard-working, who will recognise the constraints under which teachers work, and who will do their best to provide effective learning experiences for the children. They like students who are prepared to work hard and occasionally release the class teacher to get on with other things. Having a student like this can be a pleasure and a great help in the busy world of the school. The highest praise for students is when a school tells the college: 'If only we had a job vacant, we would like to offer it to her when she finishes the course.'

On your first teaching experience, there will be a limit to what the school will expect of you. In later practices, expectations will develop and deepen until, by the final practice, you will be doing most of what a full-time professional does. However, some class teachers are not very good at discriminating between different stages of a training course and may be unrealistic in their expectations of what you can achieve at the stage you have reached in yours. So ensure that, before the preliminary visits are over, you have spoken at length to the class teacher you will be working with, going through the course guidelines together and coming to an agreement about your teaching commitments and the aims and objectives for the practice.

Tutors, teacher tutors and the class teacher

There are always two, and sometimes three, people who will be vital to you during your time in school:

The school's 'teacher tutor'
Your college tutor
Your class teacher

Not all schools have a teacher tutor, but if they do it will be someone on the staff (perhaps the deputy head) who is responsible for co-ordinating the student-teacher experiences which the school offers, working with college staff and other teachers to help you make the most of your practice. Sometimes teacher tutors (or 'professional tutors', as some schools call them) will hold a workshop or seminar session, perhaps once a week, in which you can evaluate your progress and discuss problems of a general kind. If there are other students on practice in the school this can be a valuable and useful occasion for swapping experiences. Remember, though, that not all schools have such a person. Especially in smaller primary schools, the role of teacher tutor is usually taken by the class teacher.

Your college tutor will also play a major role in your practice. You may know your tutor already from your course in college. It's possible, though, that your tutor will not be a full-time member of the college staff but someone employed specifically to supervise teaching practices. If that is the case, do not for a moment think that you are not going to be supervised by an expert: the kinds of people whom colleges approach for this job have often spent many years working in college themselves, or have perhaps retired recently from running their own primary schools. What's more, tutors like these often have more time to spare than busy college lecturers, who may have to see at least another three students after you before rushing back to college to give a lecture.

The tutor's responsibilities

Tutors have a variety of roles, including:

- Liaising with the school to ensure that there is a common basis of understanding between the school and the college about what is expected of you.
- Supporting you in your planning.
- Reading your teaching-practice file.
- Watching and evaluating your lessons.
- Giving you oral and written guidance about the quality and development of your work in the classroom.
- At the end of the practice, working with teachers in the school to agree on a final report – and perhaps a grade.

Tutors normally see their students only occasionally during the practice – perhaps once a week for an hour or two. This means that if you need to contact your tutor, you will have to take the initiative. If you are struggling, he or she will try to support you. If you are doing well, your tutor will help you build on your successes.

What tutors are looking for

A tutor will ask a number of questions about your preparation, attitude and the effectiveness of your classroom practice:

1. Do your preliminary schemes of work show an awareness of the particular situation in which they will be carried out? Do they show that you have thought in terms of the variety of ability within the class? Are you aiming for the achievable – and even hoping for something extra?
2. Is your daily preparation thorough and realistic? Is the purpose of a particular session clearly stated?
3. Is your classroom organisation sound? Are you aware of early finishers, fast workers, shirkers and slowcoaches? How do you deal with them? Does your planning take account of the fact that you may have to relate to individuals, to groups, and to the whole class?
4. Do you make full use of the classroom's facilities? Have you considered the practicalities of resources, making sure that you aren't planning work which requires equipment, etc. that the school doesn't possess?
5. Are your instructions clear? Do you use an appropriate tone of voice? Are you explaining thoroughly? Do you give the children an opportunity to clarify your expectations by asking them questions and receiving feedback? Do you take their comments seriously?
6. Do you use questions carefully, allowing for a variety of responses and not always merely a single 'yes/no' or 'correct' answer? Do you labour a point unnecessarily, playing a guessing game with pupils, when a simple explanation would save time? Are you giving all the children equal opportunities to respond?
7. Are the children happy with you? Is there a pleasant and constructive working atmosphere? Do the children seem fully occupied, enthusiastic, or at least not bored?
8. Are you keeping records of progress? For the class? For the groups? For the individual? For yourself?
9. Do you have a good working relationship with the other adults involved? Are you making an effort to make use of extra help if it is offered? Are you able to take advice and act on it?
10. Above all, are the children learning anything from you? And can you prove it?

We shall be examining these aspects of work in school throughout this book. In the meantime, a final thought about tutors: they have all had classroom experience. They know the sort of problems you're experiencing. They have almost certainly supervised many other students in your position. Keep your tutor well informed.

The preliminary visit

The day has come at last! Imagine yourself entering the school for the first time. Your nerves jangle and your mouth feels dry. You wonder what on earth you're doing there! Don't worry! Most students entering school as teachers feel just the same. There may even be another student going into the same school, so don't be dismayed. Once you are in school, these early nerves should quickly pass. You'll be far too busy to let anxiety cloud the experience. Check that you are properly dressed. Err on the side of formality, at least for the first visit. Few schools are strict on dress, but it's a good idea to dress in a manner which reflects that of the majority of staff. If in doubt, ask your class teacher. If you are a male in an otherwise all-female staffroom, it's sensible to stick to a jacket and tie, with clean-looking trousers. Don't allow dress to become a problem.

Just before nine o'clock on any school morning, streams of children make their way to this familiar place, lunch-boxes swinging, bags bulging with PE kit, homework and a variety of paraphernalia, sweat-shirts bearing the school motif merging into a tide of bodies. Watch them as they converge on the school. Some are so tiny it seems incredible that they can already go to school. Others seek independence from parents, scurrying ahead despite the protestations of mother or father, who struggle gamely behind with pushchair-, pram- or bag-load of boxes, pots and toilet-roll middles for topic work. The oldest children stroll nonchalantly, chattering with friends, secure in the knowledge

that they occupy the top notch in the pecking order. A bell rings. A whistle blows. The tide heaves in a sudden burst of energy, some running, others finding the comfort of friends. Last-minute kisses and hugs. Parents dissolve into the morning. A lone figure, resplendent in dark hat, fluorescent coat and heavy boots, leans a giant lollipop against the wall, sighs with relief at another job completed and turns towards home and refreshment.

Meanwhile, inside the school, children ease or scramble their way into the classrooms. Teachers' voices echo across the cloakrooms, encouraging, cajoling and welcoming. Parents are to be seen here and there, some laughing and smiling with the teacher, others standing insecurely a little way off, uncertain about their right of entrance. Yet others move confidently about, old hands who know their way, pleased to belong. The occasional word of rebuke may be heard, but the scene is largely one of anticipation at the thought of the day ahead. Gradually the hubbub fades and the doors close. Children settle at their tables or on the carpet near the teacher's desk. Registers are taken, money given for safe keeping, precious possessions admired by the teacher. Bottoms squirm on seats, faces settle, expressions concentrate. The day has begun.

You and your pupils

How are you going to cope? What is to be your attitude? Where will your responsibilities lie in all this? As the children's teacher, you will have a role to play, only part of the total picture, but an important part none the less. Your attitude and your reactions will help to shape each little person's life. Your kindness, understanding and skill in teaching may transform the desperate into the bearable. It may be that your class is, for some of the children, a haven in an otherwise stormy life.

15

Children with potential are waiting to be encouraged and inspired into achievement. The under-achiever is waiting to find that sudden spark which will ignite capability. The high-flyer will be waiting to be taken still further ahead. What difference will you be able to make? Seize the opportunity, for not many people have it.

Outside the classroom

Though it is always about children and their learning, life in school isn't all about classrooms. There are meetings, playground duty, record-keeping, corridor displays, casual encounters, parents' evenings, staff meetings, school fêtes and visits away. When you go into school, you will see only a part of the whole. Teaching involves close association with other adults: other teachers, parents, the care-taker, secretary, technician, classroom helper and visitors from outside. As a new teacher, you have entered a world full of people, all of them, in their many different ways, relying on you.

CHECKPOINTS

Is the school all you expected? Ask yourself these questions:

1. How do my preconceptions of what school is like match what I am now discovering to be the reality?
2. Does what I see outside the classroom bear any relation to what goes on within?
3. What is my position in relation to all the other adults who come to the school?
4. How does it feel to be one of the most important people in the lives of other people's children?

A meeting

Open the door and there stands the class teacher. See her noting a child's progress in her record book, adjusting a wall display, mounting paintings, writing names on the front of new exercise books, checking work, glancing hurriedly at information from the local college about next term's student teacher. She looks up and sees you there... .

2

FIRST IMPRESSIONS

The class teacher may already be occupied in her work when you first meet her. Perhaps she's speaking to a parent, another teacher or a child. She may simply be sitting quietly behind her desk. (Some teachers like to sit in silence before the session begins to calm themselves and prepare for the tide of demands which will inevitably come their way.) Whatever your first reactions may be, treat the teacher with respect and courtesy.

Some teachers feel uneasy when a new student first appears, so however nervous you may feel, try hard to seem relaxed and pleasant and show an interest in what she says. If you can, have ready some ideas of your own which you could use as the basis for conversation; don't expect the class teacher to supply them all. But find the right time for those sensible questions and intelligent practical suggestions: any student who tries to hold a serious conversation with a teacher who is half-way up a wall pinning up a display, or deep in conversation with a sobbing child, is unlikely to be well received.

Some class teachers can be over-protective of their class, failing to give the student teacher the space, time and opportunity to become accepted by the children and so to get down to useful work. If you suspect your class teacher may be like this, remember: it is her class, and she has spent many hours every day working to develop a particular atmosphere, routine and quality of relationship within it. However, by taking a student, she is implicitly offering to share the results of this work with you. So if you feel that the teacher is likely to be possessive, remind yourself why – and show your readiness to learn, to take your time, to work to her direction. Build her confidence as she must build yours. Your first aim must be to help your class teacher realise that you are likely to be a person who will be good to work with and trustworthy as a colleague.

Class teachers are people: imperfect, occasionally misjudging situations and events, finding the going tough, arriving tired and irritable on some mornings, inspired and inspiring on others. They worry, fret, strive and struggle. They glory in unexpected moments of success, their day made happy by a learning breakthrough, an unexpected step forward by a child who seemed stuck. They respond to the children's progress with attentiveness and sensitivity. They may not know all the answers, but they certainly know more of them than you. Happy the student teacher whose sympathetic, caring class teacher remembers well the pressures of her own teaching practices: the sense of nervousness – even panic – which can sometimes seem overwhelming as you try to fit in, to cope, to prosper, under such scrutiny. Remember that she was once in your position. This will help both of you.

Children place their own class teacher very high in the order of importance within a school. So whether the teacher is good, bad or indifferent, she most certainly is not insignificant.

'Find the right time for those intelligent suggestions.'

The class teacher at work

There are two areas in which you can gain from closely observing your class teacher:

Her style and personality.
The strategies she uses in organising and managing the classroom activities.

They are, of course, related, but as you make your observations, try to separate them mentally.

Style and personality

- How does the teacher enter the room and establish her presence?
- Where does she position herself in the room?
- How does she address the children?
- How does she like to be addressed by them?
- What does she insist on?
- What does she tolerate?
- What makes her cross?
- What makes her smile and laugh?
- How does she cope with noise or disturbance?
- How does she react to individual children?

As you observe the class teacher at work, try to grasp the principles which motivate her actions and behaviour. See how she influences the class and how they influence her.

Look at the way she enters the classroom at the start of a session. Here she is, outside the door. She may have a gaggle of children clustering about her or she may be alone. (This in itself might tell you something about her relationship with the children.) Watch again: does she sweep – or creep – into the room? Does she walk briskly, or plod? Does she stand upright and confident? Would you say that her mind was concentrated on the task in hand, or far away?

Once in the room, notice the way she stands. Where are her hands? Certainly not defensively entwined around her body or twiddling her hair or rubbing the back of her neck. She uses them as another tool, gesticulating, pointing, describing, supporting. She looks around, taking in the scene. Does she try to face children directly when she listens to them? Does she seem really interested? Does she respond to what she sees, or does she fail to see what's going on? If so, might this be

19

intentional? (Sometimes it is sensible to ignore certain things in order to concentrate on others.)

CHECKPOINTS

1. Does the class teacher insist on all the children being in their seats, or on the carpet, or standing still, or engaged in some work? (What seems to be the pattern?)
2. Does she call across the room, or approach individuals and speak to them separately in a normal tone?
3. How does she use her voice to control the situation?
4. Does she stand rooted to the spot, giving orders like a ringmaster in a circus?
5. Does she move rapidly from place to place attending to each situation in turn?
6. Does she edge round the perimeter of the room, interacting with the children as little as possible?
7. Does she uses strong eye-contact in preference to movement or voice?

She probably does all these things at different times. A skilful teacher will match her approach to the situation. For instance, the 'ringmaster' position may be the most appropriate when a teacher is trying to organise large numbers of children in a complex activity (during a PE or drama lesson, for instance, or on the way to assembly). But if that were the only way she positioned herself, she would be missing other useful strategies. Sometimes, edging round the perimeter of the room might suggest that a teacher is hesitant, even afraid to become involved with the learning going on there. At others, however, it could be the best place to be: for instance, when children (alone or in groups) have been given tasks to do and where the constant intervention of the teacher could interrupt and distract them. As you watch the way your class teacher creates the atmosphere at the beginning of the session, try to see how she matches her approach to the particular kinds of learning going on at the time.

How does the teacher speak to the class – as a whole, and as a group of individuals? Listen to the expressions she uses and her natural tone of voice:

- 'Sit down, everybody!'
- 'Let's have a bit of hush!'
- 'By the time I count to three I want everybody in their seats. One, two... .'
- 'Why aren't you ready?'
- 'Everyone stop what they're doing and look at me.'
- 'Hands on heads...on shoulders...on knees... .'
- 'Well done, Barbara, you've got straight down to work without me having to tell you!'

Do the children respond immediately or are some of them ignoring her? Is there a child who feigns obedience yet subtly creates even more disturbance? How long is the teacher prepared to wait until she has the attention of each child in the class? Does she smile, make a joke, scowl and get angry? Does she repeat her command, raise her voice, call out the name of an individual, threaten, cajole, rebuke, encourage? Does she use a particular event to make generalisations...

- 'If people made a bit more effort to move around quietly, we wouldn't have all this noise!'

or blow her top...

- 'Will you sit down, now! I've never known such a dreadful racket!'

or use mild sarcasm...

- 'If you can't be quieter than that, Eddie , I'll have to buy you a pair of slippers to wear in the classroom!'

or say nothing and wait for things to settle, refusing to respond to any child, staring hard around the room at individuals, raising her eyebrows from time to time? Look at her eyes. Notice how she picks up the child whose thoughts are elsewhere. See her intense eye-contact with that child, then the firm-but-friendly speaking of his name, the acknowledging nod and 'Thank you' as he concentrates his attention.

Listen to her voice. Is it sweet and mellow, enthusiastic but controlled, eager but in no hurry? Consider the volume: she begins by speaking in a low tone, clear and relaxed. Watch the children lean forward slightly to catch her words, as she convinces them by her intonation that this is something worth listening to. She makes the dullest instruction come to life. Every situation is different, and she will match the form of her address to the needs of the moment.

The opening minutes of the session are useful indicators, then, of the way a professional teacher goes to work. The way she stands and the way she talks are vital means of establishing and maintaining the right relationship with the class. She will modify her style to suit the circumstances: the class will need quite different handling in a session following playtime on a wet day and a sunny day, for example.

CHECKPOINTS

In general, see whether your class teacher's approach could be described in these terms:

1. Entering in a positive frame of mind.
2. Scanning the room/area and being alert to potential opportunities and difficulties.
3. Choosing the most appropriate tactic for bringing the class to order and establishing authority in the situation.
4. Being ready to smile, laugh, show pleasure – and annoyance – where appropriate.
5. Avoiding arrogance, smugness, unkindness or personal vendettas.
6. Making every effort to give the class a feeling of security through her presence and her actions.
7. Speaking in a clear, confident natural way.

This picture of the class teacher won't be true for every one, or for any teacher all the time. Perhaps yours has a different approach. You will need to watch carefully and think hard about it. How will your own approach correspond or differ? It is certainly not a good idea to mimic your class teacher; you must find your own natural style. But doing so will come more easily if you observe a professional.

Strategies: organising the classroom

You can learn much about the way your class teacher works by seeing how she has organised her classroom. Take a good look around the room and adjacent areas. Find out where the equipment is kept.

'It is not a good idea to mimic your class teacher.'

Obvious things like pencils, spare paper, construction kits and plasticine are particularly important. Are the items identified by a clearly written label or an old, messy one? This in itself will tell you something about the classroom where you are going to work. Even if it does look a little worn, you can be sure that the teacher knows where everything is. After a while, she will expect you to know as well, so keep your eyes open. It may be worth producing a rough sketch, or even a detailed plan view of the room, including the placing of tables, chairs, etc. Consider the accessibility of the equipment for the children. Such a plan will familiarise you with your surroundings and help you learn where the children belong in the classroom. It can also be really valuable when you get back to college and are trying to remember where everything was.

Self-sufficiency

Notice to what extent the children are self-sufficient in their work. What happens if they want to borrow a rubber, use a scrap piece of paper or play with a jigsaw? This will link closely with the way in which the teacher organises the sessions. Some teachers like children to be self-sufficient and show initiative. Others are stern with a child who tries to do so, seeing him as taking advantage, and insist that every

23

action is agreed with them first. Be observant about the access allowed. If, when you begin your time in school, you permit the children to behave differently, they will quickly relish the new-found freedom and may begin to exploit it. The class teacher will expect you to enforce the rules, so check any uncertainties you have with her.

Grouping and organisation

More vital lessons can be learned about the class teacher's approach by seeing how she organises the pupils during the school day. How does she group them for different activities? This can vary from a situation where the whole class is involved with an activity at the same time, through groups of children working at different tasks, to individuals working on various things independently. Most teachers use several approaches to grouping in their classroom organisation. Aim to continue a similar pattern of working when you join in.

Changing activities

Equally important will be to watch the way in which the teacher moves from one mode of teaching to another. If children are occupied with a variety of different activities in a single class-setting (as is often the case in the early years), the key to the development of a settled system will be the movement of children between activities. If a whole-class approach is being used (more common with older children), the movement is more likely to involve a change of mode for the teacher.

Take, for example, a class of five-year-olds who are working on the theme 'People who help us'. During this particular session, a group of eight children are working at two tables with a helper, who is showing them how to cut and stitch pieces of felt for a collage. The class teacher herself is on the carpet, talking with a similar-sized group about the visit they are going to make to a nearby police station in a few days' time. She is asking questions which encourage the children to respond and share their thoughts and concerns. She wants to be sure that they understand the purposes for going, and don't have any anxieties. The exchanges are fairly animated and noisy, in contrast to the quiet concentration of the first group. Two other groups are operating at the same time: three children sit listening to a story on tape through headphones, following the story in a shared book, and a fourth group of five competent older children are composing a letter to the nurse who came into school yesterday to tell them about her work. As you watch, the story comes to an end and the three children who were listening take off their earphones and wander across to the class teacher, informing her that 'We've finished' (dreaded words!). How does the class teacher cope? Does she:

- Tell them to go and choose from a range of existing activities?
- Ask them if they've got any Maths to finish?
- Invite them to sit with the group and listen to what they're discussing (even though they've heard it already)?
- Hand them a worksheet to colour?
- Suggest that they select a task from the list of 'Things to be done'?

Whatever the response, the chances are that, within a few moments, this group of children will be engaged in a new task while the class teacher is still occupied with her original group. It is the children who are changing their activity, and not the teacher.

By contrast, here is a class of nine-to-ten year olds listening to the class teacher describing the appalling conditions that the early polar explorers had to endure. She graphically and accurately details their deprivations and sacrifice, occasionally quoting from a text she carries with her as she moves around the room. The children follow her with their eyes and ears as she creates this grim picture. She is well-informed and has obviously read widely. She refers to an exhibition of 'Early Settlers in America' the class visited a couple of months earlier, reminding them of some of the problems those people faced, and of the tales of heroism and injustice which characterised those harsh days. You realise that the class has been sitting quietly up to this point. You are impressed that the teacher has held their attention and caused them to think deeply.

The teacher pauses and waits. She stands perfectly still, but says nothing, merely looking around the room. To your surprise, hands begin to be raised, and after a few moments she speaks a name and looks towards that child. He comments on something he saw on television last night about explorers. The teacher nods and thanks him. She speaks another name ... and the process continues. You wonder how she can elicit a response with such apparent ease, then realise that this is a regular pattern of conversation in her class. The children have become used to listening to the teacher quietly and having their own comments valued in turn. Within five minutes several exchanges have taken place. The teacher, who a short time before had been the centre of attention, seems now to be a mere onlooker as the children dictate the pace of the discussion.

Finally the teacher cuts in, thanking everyone for their contributions. She produces a series of tasks which require groups of children to work together. The tasks are similar, but each has a specific focus. A new form of organisation is required; tables have to be moved, groups sorted, explanations given. Instead of being a ringmaster in the circus, our teacher is moving briskly about, answering a string of questions, clarifying the tasks. The atmosphere of the room has changed; the format is different. The teacher's role has altered accordingly.

The successful class teacher, then, is able to modify the organisation of her classroom to allow a range of different activities, matching the format to the nature of the children's learning. Sometimes, she will be the centre of attention for the whole class. At other times, she will slip into the background, leaving the children free – either alone or in groups – to concentrate on their work. Over a day in your own classroom, watch how the patterns of organisation change.

CHECKPOINTS

1. Can you see a pattern in the way the teacher organises activities in the class?
2. How does her organisation allow for the unexpected?
3. How does she allocate children to groups?
4. How much does her own behaviour vary during one session?
5. How much do the pupils' activities vary over the same period?
6. How does the teacher control changes of activity?
7. Does the mood of the class alter at these moments of change?

Other people

Everything the class teacher does involves other people. You will see her working with her colleagues when she takes you into the staffroom. Perhaps a parent will drop in while you are observing her lessons; watch the way she handles the situation. Other adults, too, may come and go as the day progresses, each one approaching the class teacher in one of her many roles. But what of those twenty or thirty people who are with her all the time? What can you learn as you get to know the children?

THE CHILDREN

When you first enter a classroom, you are stepping into someone else's territory, an area of great importance to the children who work there with their teacher every day. This is increasingly obvious as the children grow older: for some upper juniors, the classroom is seen as a space to be protected and guarded. Younger children don't express this protectiveness as openly, but the feeling is there none the less.

Within that territory of the classroom lives a small society. Over the preceding weeks and months, patterns of behaviour have been created.

'The classroom is seen as a place to be protected and guarded.'

A pecking order has been established among the children. Members of this society know by now which child is the most able, the most vulnerable, the most easily impressed, the most unco-ordinated and the bossiest. They have seen their teacher deal with awkward situations and watched the negotiations which characterise classroom life. They have observed her responding, triumphing, fretting, relaxing, labouring. They have detected her moods, spotted her weaknesses, probed her sensitivities, and seen what makes her happy. Some events have stayed in the children's memories. They may have shared them with their parents, friends and relatives. Their teacher will, by now, be known as 'good', 'lovely', 'friendly' or 'horrible'. Favourites have been selected, work patterns established and friendships or rivalries cultivated. Each child has sensed how the teacher responds not only to him or her but to other children in the class, to adult helpers, to visiting parents, to the presence of the headteacher – and now to you.

You enter this complex web of interaction, friendship, conflict and strongly-felt relationships. The children look up. They focus on you. They are used to adults around the place, but you are different. You are to stay in the classroom with them and become part of the life and working of the school. You will have to be accommodated as a new thread in its fabric. Who are you? What are you like? Where do you fit in? How important are you? Such questions quickly form in the children's minds.

The children speak to you and you respond. One pupil smiles sweetly, another scowls, another ignores you, another demands your immediate attention – and of course you respond. The initiation has begun: you are being absorbed into the rites and culture of the classroom. The children are weighing you up, establishing the boundaries. This is a necessary part of establishing any new social pattern. However, the classroom differs from many other situations because you are an adult and almost everyone else is a child. This in itself marks you out as significantly different. But it goes further for, once established as the children's student teacher, you will gain power, opportunity and responsibility not shared by other adults. Especially for the older student it may require a positive effort to realise that days spent, say, as a mother helping out in school, or as a classroom assistant, are now superseded by a more privileged but onerous position. Some students never find their momentum during teaching practice because they fail to grasp the significance of the move from being simply an adult in a world of children to being *the* adult.

Taking responsibility

We all like to be liked, and it helps her greatly if a teacher is popular with the children. Qualities of fairness and good humour are admired by almost everyone. There is, though, a world of difference between being approachable and reasonable and being an elder brother or sister or an auntie or uncle figure. To show unreserved enthusiasm for a child's preoccupations may win short-term approval, but it will quickly be replaced by a lack of respect. Within a short time there will be work to complete, schedules to meet, tidying-up to be finished. The children have to do their jobs, pick up mess, stand still, listen attentively, respond to orders – and they may not want to. You will then have to change roles suddenly, to become the person in charge. The child receiving the instruction, demand or request from you may be the very child you were pals with only a short time before. Now what? The chances are that you will have to be more insistent than you wished, using your adult power and experience as weapons in a conflict in a way that undermines the relationship you were hoping to build. You must expect these challenges. Don't be surprised or worried by them: all new teachers undergo a similar initiation. Throughout these early times in the classroom, be prepared to undergo this 'testing'.

CHECKPOINTS

1. When might the children consider that you are intruding?
2. What allowances are you making for the fact that the children will be keeping you under close scrutiny?
3. What message will the children relay home about you?
4. How can you help to ensure that the children perceive you as a 'real teacher'?
5. What is the best way to gain the children's respect?

Your class

During the first couple of days, as you settle in and get to know the children better, make notes under the following headings, being as specific as you can:

1. General skills
2. Subject skills
3. Attention span and concentration
4. Pupil autonomy
5. Equal opportunity

1. General skills

To a large extent children's general skills depend on their age. Can they handle scissors, hold a pencil correctly, draw a straight line with a ruler, catch a ball, rub out without creasing a page? If some or all of the class lack certain skills, for want of practice or through ignorance, it gives you an immediate starting-point for your teaching. Don't be afraid to pinpoint the areas which require attention and concentrate on them with the class. It may seem trivial to you that some children can't sharpen a pencil, but it makes a big difference to them.

2. Subject skills

Each subject will demand a range of specific skills. For instance, the skills associated with Mathematics would be enough to keep you busy throughout the practice. Can the pupils handle equipment correctly, discuss ways of solving problems, and use multiplication tables? Make a note of some of the skills needed in different parts of the curriculum. Art: can the pupils mix colours? English: can they talk together in groups? When using reference books, do they turn pages correctly? Technology: can they switch the computer off and on? Music: can they hold a tambourine in the right way?

Your task is to get an idea of your pupils' skills, so begin by focussing on some of the significant ones, then prepare or modify your plans accordingly. Of course, the abilities of the children in the class will vary. In the average class of ten-year-olds, there may be a few children operating at the intellectual levels of significantly younger or older children. Some children who excel in, say, reading and writing may be poor at practical activities such as clay work. So don't assume anything, but observe. There is no simple answer to judging the ability level of a class, or of an individual, though you should be able to gain a general impression of the situation in the first few days.

3. Attention span and concentration

As you begin to teach the class, notice when the children's attention is secured, when it is wavering and when it is impossible to sustain. Spot the times when children are bored, restless or dispirited. There are many possible reasons, including such things as a poor night's sleep or a coming birthday party, but often it is because their attention or concentration span have been exceeded.

In little children, irregular behaviour may signal fatigue or boredom. They may begin to yawn, spin around on their chairs, whisper, play with their hair, gaze into the distance, put their hands in the air, go to sleep sitting up, sing to themselves, or even stand up without warning and head for home. Older children are more subtle, but the theatrical yawn, feigned falling off a seat, asking a question to change the subject or deviate from the task in hand are all familiar signs of boredom.

Don't be dismayed but do be watchful and decide how such behaviour might be avoided or acted upon. The degree to which a child is willing to persevere depends to a large extent on the work you set, your personality, and your ability to hold the attention of the class.

4. Pupil autonomy

Some children are naturally bold and willing to exercise initiative. Others are timid and need encouragement. Others still are lazy or disorganised. In the same way, teachers have different views on the way children should behave and respond in the classroom. Take time to notice the different reactions of the children. Are there some who always volunteer (and perhaps often get chosen) while others sit passively? Does the class appear to know the whereabouts of the basic resources? Is there emphasis on 'helping yourself', or does every decision pass through the teacher? Are there possibilities for teaching-points here, or at least for encouraging and fostering particular classroom procedures? If you are able to train and encourage children to become self-sufficient, it will help you greatly, and relieve you of having to stop constantly to attend to minor things that the children could do for themselves. It is a simple thing, for instance, for young children to assist one another with putting on an apron for painting. Again, responsibility for taking and returning equipment can be delegated to a child or a group of children. However, make it clear to the children where they must not act without your supervision.

5. Equal opportunity

Teachers' differing attitudes towards boys and girls have been much discussed in recent years. You will have been persuaded that every child is entitled to full access to curriculum opportunities. The notion that some activities are appropriate exclusively to either boys or girls is one that has been challenged, leading schools to formulate their policy for equal opportunities. Is this philosophy evident in the classroom? How much effort is made to ensure fairness?

Although there are bound to be some children who are more like-able than others, your principal task will be to teach all of them effectively, which means giving them all the appropriate amount of attention. It is easy to fall into the habit of giving some children too much attention at the expense of others; to smile and respond positively to some but not to others; to dismiss particular children with superficial comments and reserve your lavish praise for the few. Children soon notice this pattern of behaviour and interpret it as favouritism, which it is.

Finally, be careful of other messages that can be passed to the children:

- Who gets the first go at exciting things?
- Does any child seem always to be last?
- Which children are placed together?
- Do the less able end up with the poorest resources?
- Does the loudest child get his or her own way?
- Are some children excluded from activities by their group?

Some children really do require special help and attention due to their learning difficulties. As a professional trainee, you will need to exercise careful judgement here, balancing individuals' special needs with the challenge of giving each child a fair proportion of your time.

The way children learn

The teacher who can work *with* the child's natural capacity to learn seems likely to achieve greater success than the one who works *against* it. But how do children learn? This is a most important question. You cannot hope to be effective as a teacher until you understand how children learn. Here are some ideas, based on an article by Barth (1975).*

* Barth,R.S. (1975) 'Open education: assumptions about children, learning and knowledge in *Curriculum Design*, editors Goldby, M. Greenwald, J. and West, R. London, Croom Helm in association with Open University Press.

How do you respond to them – and why?

1. Children are naturally curious and will explore situations without the need of adult support.

There may be insufficient time to allow endless exploration, however. Sometimes you need to channel this curiosity into tasks and activities that you wish to develop.

2. Exploratory behaviour will inevitably lead to meaningful discovery.

You have the responsibility to ensure that the exploration is purposeful. There are times when a child needs time and space to explore ideas and if you intervene too quickly you may prevent useful discoveries from being made, but if you delay too long the children could waste time. You will need to be watchful and exercise your judgement.

3. Children will learn best if they are in a secure environment.

If you have made your expectations clear to the children and explained what is acceptable and what is not, and if the purpose of the activity is clear, they should be able to learn in a relaxed yet purposeful manner. Children need to feel that what they are doing is allowed. Fear of the teacher's disapproval can hinder creativity and enterprise.

4. Children need confidence in themselves if they are to reach their full potential.

If your approach to children is characterised by negative comments, and if you make it plain that you expect little from them, you will create self-doubt in their minds, leading to under-achievement. Keep your remarks positive and encouraging. Tell the children that you believe they can succeed. If they don't achieve as much as you hoped for, congratulate them on what they have done and prepare the ground for future endeavour by stressing that, next time round, it will be even better. Give the children something to look forward to.

5. A rich environment, offering a wide array of materials and resources, facilitates children's learning.

Resources and materials alone will not ensure learning, though how they are used might. Children need proper training in the use of equipment. Careless use of materials leads to wastage and disappointment for others in the class who wish to use them, so establish a procedure for distribution and sharing.

6. Play is indistinguishable from work as the predominant mode of learning in early childhood.

The importance of play in learning has been widely debated. It is important to be sure that you understand the meaning of the term 'play' in the context of learning. In the early-years classroom, play is normally taken to mean that children are not closely supervised and can use resources (such as construction materials or dressing-up clothes) as their imagination prompts them. One of the criticisms of play as a method of teaching, however, is that it is used by teachers to keep children occupied without sufficient thought as to the learning which may be taking place. If you allow children to play in this way, think hard about how you can justify it to yourself, to the class teacher and to parents. Parents sometimes complain that their child has 'only been playing' at school. They could be right.

7. Children have both the competence and the right to make significant decisions concerning their own learning.

Most of the preparation and planning of lessons is your responsibility. However, there are times when the children have ideas of their own which may contribute too. When you explain your intentions to the class, it can be a good idea to ask them for their own suggestions as well. (This is particularly important when they are involved in a problem-solving exercise in Science, Technology, or Mathematics.) If the ideas they suggest are not practical, offer thanks and praise anyway; don't dismiss genuine suggestions out of hand.

8. If a child is fully involved and enjoying what he or she is doing, learning is taking place.

Children can be involved and enjoying themselves without learning anything. However, it is true that if a child is motivated by the task and experiencing satisfaction, learning is much more likely than when they are not. You can help to make learning interesting by presenting the lesson in an imaginative and unusual way. One student teacher introduced a project about air to some nine-year-olds by telling them an exciting story of a parachute drop. He went on to ask them to design a parachute, selecting from a variety of materials. Another student teacher captured her seven-year-olds' imagination during a project about the weather by showing them a short extract from the opening sequence of *The Wizard of Oz*, in which Dorothy is caught up in a whirlwind. This led to discussion and to various pictures, paintings and written work. These students had realised that it is possible to make learning fun and purposeful at the same time.

9. Collaboration is a natural outcome from two or more children being interested in the same thing and enhances learning for both of them.

There are times for children to work alone, on a piece of written work or a painting, for example. There are times for them to work in small groups of three or four, during Drama or perhaps in a practical Science activity. And there are times for whole-class collaboration; for example, preparing an assembly. Children can learn much from working together, including caring, sharing, and co-operating. However, you must not assume that this will work smoothly or automatically. Merely dividing children into groups for an activity is not enough. You must ensure that they all know the purpose of the task, and that each one is able to contribute. Look out for those children who sit and watch, or become bored because others in the group refuse to let them contribute. If children argue over who is in charge or who should be taking the initiative, try appointing a leader for a given time or delegating tasks within the group.

10. Children will naturally wish to share their discoveries with others.

There may not always be time for every child to cover each activity on offer. Many interesting discoveries and good pieces of work deserve wider recognition within the class. So consider the value of bringing all the children together at the end of the day to share their work with each other. This reinforces learning and gives an indication of the standards you expect. It also gives you the opportunity to make positive and encouraging comments.

The extent to which you agree or disagree with the above observations will determine how you organise learning within the classroom. For instance:

• If you are firmly convinced that children will learn effectively only if they control their knowledge and understanding, you will give them plenty of opportunity to find things out for themselves. But you will then have to limit the information and guidance you offer them.

- If you believe that enthusiasm is the key to learning, you may avoid the tasks which are less popular with the children. You may find, however, that you are neglecting to teach them important things because you sense the children aren't very enthusiastic about them.

- If you see collaboration as the best way to work, you will ensure that children with similar enthusiasms have the chance to work together. But if you never place different children together, you may miss out on potentially useful groupings.

- If you believe that it is important to have silence and the full attention of the whole class, you will organise things so that the children concentrate on what you are saying to them. This is most likely to happen when the whole class is working on the same thing at the same time. But then you will deny the children all the advantages that working in (sometimes noisy) groups can offer them.

How will you solve these problems? How will you ensure the best approach? There is little point in having grand ideas about organising learning in the classroom if the children aren't used to a particular approach or feel threatened by its novelty. In the same way, it would be a strange exercise to fill a previously bare room with a variety of resources and expect the children automatically to take advantage of them. Watch how the class teacher handles things, fit in, and gradually develop your own ideas as you discuss things with her. Teachers use a variety of approaches, depending on the circumstances.

How far should you push?

Teacher intervention strongly influences the pattern of working in the classroom. Though some children prosper given plenty of freedom of choice and the chance to explore with the minimum of help, most require more support and direction from the teacher. This is where the teacher's judgement is critical. When should you leave things alone and when should you press the child?

Imagine a situation where a five-year-old has had many opportunities to explore the use of colours in painting. Paints have been mixed and sloshed, dabbed, swirled and splattered, sometimes too runny, sometimes too dry. This will have given the child a real opportunity to acquire an elementary understanding of the nature of paints, surfaces, brushes, and techniques. But what it will not have done is to allow for an ordering of this understanding and this is where you may need to intervene.

Compare the unsophisticated free play of the five-year-old with the careful observational drawing of the nine-year-old and it is obvious that children change as they grow older. Has the child progressed this way naturally, did her teacher influence her progress, or was her progress the result of both? Educational thinkers like Jean Piaget have suggested that children cannot develop beyond a certain point until they are ready to do so. This notion of 'readiness' has been misinterpreted by some people, who have claimed that teachers damage children's progress by encouraging them to press on too soon to greater levels of achievement. While it is perfectly true that an inappropriate level of work is not going to help a child, it is equally true that the skill and encouragement of a teacher can lead a child to unexpected heights of achievement, as long as the work is matched to the child's developing abilities.

'Unexpected heights of achievement ...'

Some have claimed that teacher intervention is unnecessary and harmful to the child's 'natural' progress, but this is to misunderstand the teacher's role. Your task is to assist the education and development of the child in whatever way is appropriate. It is a delicate balance between overwhelming the child in your eagerness to help, and standing back to give him or her the opportunity to explore a task. There is a difference between the teacher who leaves it all to natural development, and the one who makes a careful decision not to press too far at a given stage in a child's learning. Both of those approaches contrast with that of the teacher who presses on regardless of the child's aptitude and readiness to learn.

Matching the pace at which each child should move is a sensitive task, particularly since a child will move at different speeds depending on the subject, his or her mood at the time, and many other circumstances. Put thirty children together in the same class and you can see how skilful a good teacher must be in maintaining each child's momentum against the forward movement of the class as a whole.

Praise and encouragement

The need to praise and encourage is important in teaching. Unfortunately, some children simply don't achieve what is hoped for. How do you encourage them? You should make it clear that you value who the child is, not merely what the child can do. To praise a piece of work implies that it is superior to other similar work. This may help the individual but it could discourage others who are unable to match that quality. On the other hand, to encourage is to foster self-respect and co-operation. It reassures children that it isn't *the* best that you are looking for, but *their* best.

For example, some of the clay models made by a group of eight-year-olds will stand out as being superior. You might find yourself describing each of them with a superlative but, after praising them like this, the praise loses its impact. The children will tell you whose model is the best if you ask them. Appropriate though it is to give the best examples strong praise, *every* model should have something to commend it. There are many ways of encouraging those children who haven't made such good models. You can praise them for persevering, or point out the most satisfactory part of the model, or tell them you are pleased they have tried so hard despite finding the work difficult.

Being encouraging does not mean going about with blinkers on, oohing and aahing at every half-baked effort. On the contrary, it develops a relationship that allows a genuine dialogue between you and the child about the merits of the piece of work and the child's progress. A series of questions may be helpful:

'Which is your favourite part?'
'Are you happy that this is your best?'
'If you had a chance to start again, would you do anything differently next time?'
'Remember that piece of work you did last Tuesday? Do you think this is as good?'
'Were you here when we discussed using a coloured border around the work?'

The child's response is often sufficient in itself to promote a positive discussion. The use of a blanket term like 'good' may not be appropriate. Being specific is far more constructive:

'I like the way you've used two different colours.'
'You've done well to develop the ideas we discussed.'
'That's an excellent idea for shaping the wheels.'
'I like the way you end the story.'

CHECKPOINTS

1. Are you clear about the variety of approaches which may be suitable for the children?
2. Which teaching approaches are you likely to use most often?
3. How will you know if children are doing their best?
4. How far are you willing to let children try things for themselves?
5. How will you encourage high standards of work?

Children who present a challenge

As you get to know your class, you will realise that every child has a different character and responds to you in different ways. The individuality of children is part of the enjoyment and challenge of the job.

However, there are always a few children in every class who present particular challenges. Every teacher finds herself spending a lot of time with such children. Be prepared to meet children like these:

Debbie

Debbie is eight years old, large for her age, and the youngest child of three. In her academic work, she rarely excels, though her reading and general understanding are adequate. In class she is normally quiet, working in a steady if unspectacular manner. The challenge for the class teacher is in Debbie's relationship with other members of the class. She has no close friends and has long been rejected by the majority of the children, who describe her as 'a nuisance' and 'smelly' (both of which are sometimes true). Debbie is constantly on the fringe of trouble. Because of her large size, she can knock children over in the playground. Such is her pleasure when she is included in a playground game that she can get very silly and spoil things; this leads to a string of complaints from the other children and equally forthright rebuttals from Debbie. In short, as she grows older and becomes ever more conscious of her limited influence as a member of the normal social scene, Debbie relies increasingly upon her ability to be loud, vulgar and silly to gain some sense of status within the school community. This behaviour and attitude spill over into the classroom, affecting group work and collaborative activity. To avoid the humiliation of rejection, Debbie claims that she doesn't want to work with others, but would rather work alone. The teacher is becoming desperate to find someone to work with Debbie and could be forgiven for agreeing to Debbie's request rather than constantly persuading others to accommodate her.

Some questions:
1. Where do you think Debbie's rejection might have begun?
2. How can the class teacher encourage other children to include her in group activities?
3. Most importantly, how can she be helped to grow in self-esteem?

These are difficult questions for experienced and inexperienced teachers alike. It's true that some children are not particularly easy to like or admire. Teachers secretly have sympathy with the others, who keep such children at arm's length. Yet the teacher must do something or the situation will only get worse. Establishing a friendly relationship with Debbie will have a twofold effect. Firstly, it will help to raise the child's self-esteem. Secondly, the other children, wanting to remain on good terms with the teacher, will to some extent reflect her attitude. Praising Debbie in front of them will raise her self-esteem still further. The teacher could also confide in some of the children with whom she has a good relationship her concern that Debbie seems 'a bit sad at being left out', and try to enlist their support.

Jamal

Jamal is ten years old but looks older. He is an only child from a well-to-do family. He receives a good deal of money from various sources, including an indulgent grandmother, but he gets no real attention from anyone. His parents often go out without him, leaving the grandparents to babysit. Jamal therefore stays up late on many occasions and rarely goes without anything he wants. He speaks loudly, boasts often, and flaunts his gadgets and knick-knacks around school. In the playground, Jamal is constantly wrapped up in his desire for status, often yelling, telling someone off aggressively with a few harshly spoken words, or walking into school too slowly or too quickly, depending upon his mood. Mealtime staff view his behaviour with apprehension and keep a comfortable distance. Inside the classroom, Jamal is unpredictable. He rarely settles to work and complains of boredom or not understanding. He responds well to careful explanation from the teacher, jealously guarding such special relationships with her by warning off any other child wandering too close to the table. This inevitably causes the teacher to rebuke him, at which point he switches off and stares away. Academically he struggles, though he occasionally pretends that he knows a lot by relaying a series of facts about an obscure subject with a good deal of apparent authority. Generally, Jamal is a dissatisfied, restless boy, who seems unhappy with life, sheltering behind a bluff exterior. Staff in the school are heard to refer to him as 'a pain'.

Some questions:
1. What is the main cause of Jamal's moodiness?
2. How can he be encouraged?
3. Where do his interests lie?

The teacher might suspect that Jamal needs more love and attention from his parents. Despite all her efforts to motivate and befriend him, he seems to take advantage of her kindness without reciprocal improvement in his attitude or conduct. He is likely to be an underachiever, and perhaps this is a possible clue to the way forward. If the teacher can convince herself that he is capable of more, she may then be able to convince him by encouragement, setting realistic and interesting tasks for him, and clarifying her expectations of him. She may want to use any interests that he has as a basis for promoting a greater enthusiasm for his work. She may need to be flexible here if more obvious strategies seem to have failed. Boys like Jamal appear intimidating at times, but they are often scared and insecure themselves.

Yasmin

Yasmin is six years old and appears unwilling or unable to respond to the class teacher's approaches. She seems much older than her years, often repeating adult-sounding phrases. She can hold her own in classwork, but rarely excels, and will suddenly refuse to complete a task. Attempts by the teacher to get close to her are usually met by a hurtful, confusing lack of response. Occasionally, this barrier will be breached and for a fleeting moment Yasmin's enthusiasm will come bursting through. Most of the time, however, she maintains her enigmatic distance. Her relationship with the other children causes difficulties. They are afraid of her and disturbed by her unpredictable nature. Numerous incidents have occurred both inside and outside the classroom, usually resulting in injury to another child. Yasmin scratches and pinches other children. Neither telling off nor reasoning make much difference.

Some questions:
1. How can Yasmin be encouraged to develop good relationships?
2. How can the teacher help her to develop self-control?
3. What is Yasmin's greatest single need?
4. How can the teacher avoid becoming discouraged?

For such a young child, Yasmin has gone a long way towards being beyond the control of the conventional school setting. She will require much patient care and firmness. The teacher will need to keep matters under control by giving her a regular work-pattern with an exciting range of activities. Small rewards like stickers and stars may help. Confrontation should be avoided and the teacher should try to stress positive aspects of her work and attitude as often as possible. She may need to do this casually, as children like Yasmin can react against too much public praise; in any case, they will see through any insincerity. Remember, Yasmin has had six years of learning how to handle a variety of adults. Above all, she needs a patient and firm approach and the security of knowing what the teacher is prepared to accept from her, both in terms of behaviour and quality of work. The teacher will have to balance her sympathy for Yasmin against the responsibility she has to ensure that the child makes progress in her education. She should set tasks which can be completed within the limit of Yasmin's concentration but which require some effort. Substandard work should not be accepted. This will take time, and the teacher must be prepared to see little progress in the short term.

Adam

Adam is five and obviously a very bright boy. At three years old he terrorised the mothers at playgroup by his antics, including swinging where no one had swung before, climbing where it seemed impossible to climb, and raising his hand to answer every question posed during story-time, sometimes spoiling the ending by accurately predicting the outcome. He would run from the room to meet his mother, loaded with half-completed, still-wet paintings and poorly glued models, often dropping them on the floor, tripping on his laces, or creating some other form of havoc. The relief on the faces of the playgroup leaders when he left was evident to all. The home is stable and Adam is loved and well looked after, perhaps even spoiled a little, though his parents are determined that he won't become a stereotype of the only child. Once in school, Adam calmed down somewhat, but seems almost incapable of self-discipline. He cannot grasp that there is an order to life in school, and will suddenly get up and wander about or play with things as they take his fancy, without reference to anyone. When admonished by the teacher, he will only half listen before launching into an enthusiastic explanation of what he has in mind to do next. His work is always completed hurriedly and put to one side in favour of the next task. This leads to half-completed tasks and poorly presented work. The only occasion that he seems to be prepared to concentrate is on a one-to-one basis with the teacher on a reading task. This is an area in which he excels. Practical tasks are difficult for him; Adam seems to have poor co-ordination and is ungainly in his movements, despite the enthusiasm with which he attacks the job in hand. It is difficult to dislike Adam; he is hardly ever aggressive, and injures people only through his boisterous, effervescent approach to life. Several discussions have taken place with parents, who despairingly admit, 'He's just the same at home!' He has one great friend, a quiet inoffensive boy, on whom he lavishes great attention and affection.

Some questions:
1. How can the teacher harness Adam's enthusiasm?
2. When does she need to be firm?
3. How can she help him improve his co-ordination?

Adam's poor co-ordination is no one's fault, so the teacher must not unintentionally add to the weight of criticism which is probably already building up within the class. His co-ordination problems will require continuing help, but in the short term, some intensive teaching of certain skills and techniques may help to overcome them. The use of a classroom assistant could be invaluable here, but the teacher should beware of seeing this as a way of ridding herself of a problem. Adam has enthusiasm. This is a gift, and not one to be underestimated. It is clear that Adam is determined and active. He can also read well – a great advantage for any child. If Adam is to fulfil his potential, however, he will need to respond to the teacher's efforts to give him a well-structured day, allowing for his keen attitude, but preventing him from excitable excesses which lead to the kinds of situation described above. It may be that the teacher will have to be very firm, insisting on a single task being completed to her satisfaction. She must let him see that she is very interested in what he does, without being patronising. She must try to value Adam, despite the demands he makes upon her time and patience.

Sophie

Sophie is seven years old and has recently moved from a small village school to a large one in the inner city. Sophie's mother is a lively and hard-working person who is recovering from a difficult divorce case. The father does not have access to Sophie or to her older and more confident sister. The mother is anxious that Sophie gain confidence in her new surroundings. Sophie is petite and looks frail. She prefers to sit alone and rarely makes any contact with other children, who often choose her last for team games. When spoken to by the teacher, she shakes her head or looks vacantly around the room. In the playground, she plays solitary games. Her work is generally poor and she shows little initiative, sitting tight and waiting to be noticed by the teacher. The teacher succeeds in holding a conversation with her only when they are alone. She loves the classroom pet hamster and has sent her sister to ask the teacher for permission to take it home in the holiday.

Some questions:

1. How can the teacher ensure that Sophie receives appropriate attention?
2. How can she help her grow more confident?
3. How can she encourage her to work hard and succeed?

Quiet children are often overlooked in class. Louder and more confident children claim the greater part of most teachers' attention. It is important not to neglect children like Sophie. The teacher will try to ensure that she doesn't give such children only the simple tasks to complete and fail to include them in the more exciting ones. She will place them with a sensitive group who will include them in their activity. She comments on their work, even if they make little response, but is careful not to embarrass them. She gives them small jobs to do with other children to establish their self-confidence, then gradually, over two or three weeks, gives them tasks to do alone. She doesn't make a public fuss of silent children, but does show that she values them by thanking them for completing a task and expressing her belief that they have the ability to do well. In Sophie's case, the teacher must find a way of using her love for animals to stimulate interest in work, encouraging her to make an animal scrap-book, asking her about her favourite animals, telling her about her own, perhaps. Once children like Sophie realise that the teacher is trying hard to help and can be trusted, they may begin to respond positively.

All the children described above have passed through conventional schools. It is obvious that such children are likely to dominate a teacher's work (and may well be the subject of her dreams or nightmares). The success of her teaching may sometimes seem to depend on how she handles these single cases, but it is a mistake to base a teaching approach on the behaviour and responses of just one or a few children. Consider this example:

Sam

It is story-time. The class is sitting in front of you. You begin by reminding them of the story so far and asking one or two brief questions to stir their interest. You begin the story, speaking clearly and varying your tone according to the content. Sam is restless. (Sam is always restless, but seems worse today.) As you relax into the story and pick up the mood, Sam begins to squirm, and fidget, and yawn, and poke, and shuffle, and all the things Sam can do to make life difficult for you. Eventually, you stop reading and quietly mention to Sam that you are reading a story and would like everyone to sit still.

This pattern is repeated until Sam becomes unbearable. By now you have Sam sitting at your feet in an effort to restrict movement and keep the atmosphere calm. This isn't the first time that you have had to deal with such disruptiveness, of course, but you're afraid that the whole class might suffer from it. Eventually, you decide to make Sam stand in the corner of the room, away from the rest of the class, cut short the story-time (which has by now become fragmented), and set the class to work on activities you had intended to tackle after break. You speak severely to Sam after the session, and threaten exclusion from a planned outing. In fact, you consider cancelling the outing altogether if Sam has to come along, though you feel uneasy at having to consider such a course of action.

Children like Sam are always with us. If one of them turns up in your class, there are several useful questions you should ask:

1. Why is Sam restless? Is it boredom, or confusion about what is going on? Is the topic too difficult to grasp, or irrelevant? Is there some other reason (for instance, plain naughtiness)?
2. Are the rules about acceptable behaviour at story-time clear?
3. How do the other children react to Sam's behaviour?
4. Have you consulted more experienced staff about an appropriate approach and Sam's past history?
5. Are Sam's parents involved?
6. Is Sam receiving any other help outside your direct control?
7. Has your action solved the immediate problem but established fixed patterns of behaviour and response (for you, for Sam and the class)?

If Sam seems to behave badly only with you, discuss the situation with the class teacher and, if possible, watch how she deals with similar situations. You may find that Sam is simply one of those children who exasperates everyone and doesn't respond to any of the strategies employed. If you have a Sam in your class, you've got a real challenge ahead. You will need a lot of courage, patience and perseverance if you are to prosper. Nevertheless, you are the teacher, not Sam. It is your responsibility to ensure that Sam doesn't control the way you operate. It is also necessary to safeguard the welfare and progress of the other children in the class. So, *keep your cool!* Nothing is gained by getting worked up. Treat it as a challenge. Sam is just a child in your class. It's a battle of wits. You are a committed, dedicated and capable person and you have the resources to cope with Sam and to make progress. Keep a smile on your face. There are times to be deadly serious, but don't treat every misdemeanour of Sam's as though it were a major crime. Convince yourself, Sam, and the rest of the class that you are more than able to handle things. Don't give Sam too much attention. It's a fine line between ignoring events which should be noted and becoming hooked on an 'event–response' merry-go-round. Sam will have you under her thumb if you jump every time she decides to be disruptive·*

You probably considered teaching as a career because of your love for children. However, as a new teacher, you will need to go beyond a mere sentimental attachment to consider how your relationship with the children, and the quality of your teaching, can lead to their enhanced learning and maximum progress in school. So ask yourself the following questions as you develop your understanding of the way children respond – to school, to learning, to each other and to you:

CHECKPOINTS

1. Have you taken sufficient account of the complex social system existing within the classroom and your own position in it?
2. Are you responding naturally to the children's questions and demands?
3. Have you carefully noted the ability of individual children?
4. How are you encouraging autonomy and initiative?
5. What forms of praise and encouragement are you using?
6. How are you taking account of individual differences?
7. Are you giving every child a fair chance?

---

* Teachers often complain that it is boys who are the main source of disruption in the classroom; guard against unhelpful stereotypes and prejudices, however.

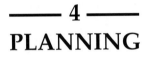

—— 4 ——
PLANNING

When you arrive at your practice school, you become an agent in a process of planning which is already well advanced. You are unlikely to have had much, if any, opportunity to be present at the planning and preparation of the programme of work arranged for the children in your class, so it is no use coming to school hoping to put your fabulous ideas into practice when the school has already decided that your class is going to do something else. Most schools are anxious to have student teachers, but only if they are prepared to co-operate. Such readiness to work with the school's ideas is even more important today than it used to be, as the demands of the National Curriculum leave teachers with less flexibility in the content of their work programmes. It's essential, therefore, to show an interest in what the school has planned and offer ways in which you can help those plans succeed.

The class teacher and planning

Within the terms of the National Curriculum, each school will have its plan for delivering the curriculum in its own way. Within this whole-school plan, your class teacher will have decided on her own approach. You will have to find out what your contribution is to be, and to do this you need to discover how the class teacher's planning works:

- How closely does the teacher refer to National Curriculum documentation?
- How far is the class teacher expected to comply with the whole-school strategy and to what extent is she able to exercise some discretion in her planning, working to her particular strengths and interests?
- How does she plan the balance across the curricular areas?
- Are certain parts of the curriculum treated as single subjects and others in an integrated form?
- What tests or assessment procedures does the school use?
- Does the class teacher use any other ways to indicate pupil progress?

Your own planning must fit in with that of the school and the class teacher. To help you plan well, you will be expected to keep a teaching-practice file, and this will become your principal planning tool as your practice progresses.

The teaching-practice file

Your college will supply you with documentation to ensure that you meet its requirements for keeping a teaching-practice file. Some of these may be quite strict, making stage-by-stage analyses of expectations; others may be more general in nature and leave you with room to manoeuvre. Do what your college asks of you; this is unlikely to differ significantly from the guidelines suggested below.

The file will be most helpful to you if it contains subsections. These could include:

- Notes about the school, including details of size and location, together with information given by the headteacher or class teacher, such as school policy documents.
- Information about the children given to you by the class teacher; full names and dates of birth, for example.
- Long-term planning.
- Lesson plans for each week, separated into days.
- Examples of worksheets and ideas for future lessons.
- Details of children's progress (samples of work, marks from tests, written comments about individuals, coverage of the National Curriculum, etc.).
- Evaluations of your own teaching, concentrating on particular lessons and also standing back (perhaps each week) and making more general comments.

Above all, remember that the teaching-practice file is yours and no one else's. Your tutor will want to see it. Your class teacher may ask to look at it as well, and so may the headteacher, but once the practice is over, no one is going to take your file away and present it to a library or raffle it for the school fund. It is a working document, which, as well as helping you make the most of the practice itself, will act as an invaluable archive as you look back and learn from your experience how to progress still further.

'The teaching-practice file is yours and no one else's.'

Long-term planning

Whether you are on a first practice, with responsibility for only one or two groups of children, or on a final practice, with responsibility for a whole class, your planning has to take into account the nature of the task. It's no use planning an ideal set of lessons in an ideal school with ideal children (we saw in the last chapter that no child is ideal). Plan flexibly for the real world so that, when things happen unexpectedly, you can adapt. Start by taking a long look at the practice. Ask yourself what you hope to have achieved by the time it finishes. This is planning for the long-term (the general strategy).

During your preliminary visits, the class teacher will have told you about the class's main area of study . For instance, it may be a History topic about Tudors and Stuarts with her class of eight-year-olds. Within this topic she may want you to concentrate on 'Voyages of discovery'. If so, you will need to think about such things as early maps and famous explorers. You will also need to take into account the children's knowledge of direction, compass readings, distance, the relative position of countries, and so on. These ideas will help you to decide where to concentrate your teaching. Having clarified these points, the next step is to find and read the relevant section of the National Curriculum documentation . In this case, the History document would be the first place to look, but don't neglect links with Geography (for instance, the location of different countries) and Mathematics (direction, mapping, etc.).

Between the time of the preliminary visits and the start of the practice you will have begun to collect ideas. Look at them hard. Think about how they might work in your situation. Write them down. Discuss them with friends, tutors and the class teacher. Be bold in your thinking! Finally, set out your learning aims for the children over the practice: what they should know, understand, and be able to do by the time it ends. Just as importantly, establish your *own* aims. What do *you* hope to be able to do, to know and to understand by the time the practice ends which you do not know, cannot do, and do not understand at present?

You need to end up with a plan that offers continuity across a period of time and takes account of: the resources available to you; the children's ability; and the way in which the class teacher organises the children. This means using existing documentation and ideas and adapting them to your own needs. It is essential to have some idea of the general direction and purpose of your learning and teaching strategy. This will act as a strong framework for your more detailed planning. Obviously, this long-term planning must harmonise with the school's and the class teacher's plans.

Weekly plans

For weekly plans, you can start to be more specific. Before the practice begins, see if you can envisage how far an idea or topic might be taken. Initially, you will only be able to visualise an outline. As the practice progresses, you can fill in the details. For example, after identifying a curriculum area, note the appropriate Attainment Level from the National Curriculum document. Look carefully at the descriptors* for that Attainment Target and write them down. Over, say, a four-week period, one descriptor could form the core of the work planned for each week. Together the four descriptors could form the basis of programme continuity, with a thorough grasp of the concept and skills associated with the first descriptor in the first week leading to work based on the second descriptor during the second week, and so on.

---

* Descriptors are the individual areas to be covered for each Level of an Attainment Target.

Check the Programmes of Study. Look to see how you can develop ideas for classroom work to match them.

Some areas of the curriculum, such as Mathematics, provide obvious continuity, but familiarity with National Curriculum documentation in the subjects you are going to teach will allow you to plan in a structured way as you become familiar with their demands. It's up to you to show how you can implement these ideas using your own initiative and imagination.

CHECKPOINTS

1. Have you consulted the class teacher about the school's long-term plans?
2. Have you looked carefully at the National Curriculum documents?
3. Are you forming an idea of the progression that the learning will follow?
4. Have you drawn up a provisional weekly timetable?

Daily planning

Once you have a clearer view of how the teaching will progress from week to week, it is time to turn to the details of what works on a daily basis. Don't attempt your daily plans until you have been through the stages described above. Only when you have gained an overview and know how the teaching and learning may develop over a period of weeks can you pin down your individual lesson plans. Otherwise these will consist of disjointed, one-off ideas which lead nowhere.

You will need to take into account the resources, abilities and grouping of the children. If you are on your first practice, dividing up the children may not apply; you may simply be given a ready-made group. Whatever the case, it is still necessary to be clear about:

• What the children have already covered (ask the class teacher).
• What they need to revise (find out what they remember).
• What you aim to achieve with them (thorough preparation).

This thoroughness is essential. For instance, every day you will need to consider such basic questions as:

'How will you explain to the children what you expect from them?'

- Are children going to be working singly or collaboratively?
- Will the work last for the time you anticipate? (Always have extra work available.)
- How will you explain to the children what you expect from them?
- Is there sufficient space for the activities?
- Are other resources, such as Maths equipment, coloured pencils and painting aprons, accessible and available, and are there enough for all the children?
- Does the classroom assistant (if you have one) know what's expected?
- What happens to the work afterwards (for example: wet paintings)?

And so on and on. Different circumstances require different levels of preparation, so you should make the process of thinking through the day from start to finish a firm habit.

Individual lessons

Each day requires the planning of individual lessons. For each lesson plan, consider subdividing a page in your file as this example:

---

1. **The purpose/aim of the session:**
   To classify minibeasts from garden soil into those that crawl and those that walk.

2. **Resources required:**
   Five shallow containers; newspaper; ten plastic spatulas; five hand-lenses; supply of small plastic tubs; reference sheet for each pair; results chart on wall.

3. **Introducing the session:**
   Read section from natural history reference book; use of close-up photograph of a centipede; asking questions arising from the last lesson to check children's recall of how to handle and identify small creatures.

4. **Structure of the lesson:**
   Introduction, followed by children working in pairs at the practical task; recording results on the chart; extension activities as needed.

5. **Activities:**
   Each pair will examine the soil sample and separate creatures into those that have/don't have legs; identify creatures with reference to the drawings on the duplicated sheet; write number of creatures observed on the class chart; carefully return creatures to their soil.

6. **What I will be doing:**
   Checking that children are taking care of the creatures and working co-operatively.
   Moving around the pairs helping with identification of creatures.
   Noting any children who seem to have difficulty with the task.

7. **Areas of the National Curriculum covered; the relevant Attainment Target(s) and Level(s).**

8. **Extension work:**
   After clearing up, produce a short list of rules for looking after tiny creatures; use the reference books to find further examples of 'helpful' and 'harmful' creatures.

9. **Links with future sessions:**
Completion of list of rules; recording findings by use of graphs; discussion about harmful and helpful creatures and the use of pesticides (links with main topic, 'Soil').

10. **Evidence that I have achieved my aim:**
The children should have worked co-operatively and recorded the results accurately; most groups should have finished the task and talked about what they discovered.

Notice again the thorough preparation that is needed. For example, it would be easy to forget the small tubs for use in separating out the creatures. Don't ruin your lesson by failing to have resources ready and spending valuable time searching for them as the children wait. Most importantly, keep the purpose of the session firmly in mind – but welcome interesting, unexpected learning opportunities if they occur. No plan should be set in concrete.

The evaluation

Your college will normally insist that you write an evaluation of your teaching sessions. This gives you an opportunity to think in detail about the way each one has gone and is an important part of teaching experience. The notion of the 'thinking teacher' or 'reflective practitioner' describes teachers who examine their own practice closely, providing both a description and an analysis of their work as a method of improving that practice. The amount you write is less important than the quality of the reflection. Comments like: 'Went really well!' or 'Disaster!' don't take you very far; in each case you need to ask 'Why?'. Some students find it helpful to write a long report to explore the heart of their teaching; others prefer to use notes. The important thing is to be specific – and honest. Here are a few starting-points to use as a basis for your evaluations:

- Times when you felt uncertain during the lesson.
- Moments of enlightenment.
- Aspects of order and discipline.
- The conduct of individuals.
- Relevance of the material.

- Whether the children seemed to enjoy the work.
- Whether you needed to modify the lesson.
- Your classroom organisation.
- Continuity and progression of the work.
- Most important of all: what the children learned.

Uncertainty often comes when you meet something new, such as your first experience of controlling the whole class, or teaching an unfamiliar subject. It can take the form of indecision in your teaching, such as when you are asked a difficult question by a child, or in a practical issue, such as when to start clearing up after a practical activity. Learn from such instances. Ask yourself:

1. Did I fail to find out some information before the lesson; for example, whether children could consult books outside the classroom?
2. Did I hesitate to confront a misbehaving child, uncertain about whether to ignore the behaviour?
3. Did I find myself poorly informed when asked a question?

Moments of enlightenment often come unexpectedly, when you see the value of using a different strategy. One student teacher commented that it had taken her weeks to realise that her approach to keeping the class quiet relied to a large extent on her saying 'Shhh!' every few seconds. Once she had realised that the strategy was obviously not working (why else would she need to repeat it every few seconds?) she explored other approaches, which she immediately put into practice. She waited until everyone was quiet and attentive, for instance.

The conduct of individuals can worry teachers. The evaluation can help you to step back and look honestly at your relationship with each child and consider whether it could be improved. Remember any bad behaviour exhibited during a day and note your response and the effect it had. Then think of another response that you might have used and whether its impact would have been different. By pinning down the types of behaviour and the way the child acts after your response, you can often detect a pattern, and finding the pattern can often be the key to improvements.

Evaluating the suitability of a lesson is very important. One of the causes of indiscipline amongst children is unsuitable work. If, after a session, you feel as if you have been in a battle and are glad to see the end of it, the children probably feel the same. If it has been an uphill struggle to motivate the children, and if they don't seem willing or able to apply themselves to the task; if their work is poor and even the hard workers don't produce satisfactory results; if the group is restless and you are constantly chiding them, consider the appropriateness of the work. On the other hand, if your lesson was a real pleasure for all concerned, it is just as important to ask the same questions to establish what helped it to succeed:

1. Were the children able to understand what you expected?
2. Did you give them opportunity to use their own ideas?
3. Did the work have a clear purpose?
4. Did you assume that all the children in the group were equally capable?

Good classroom organisation is at the heart of a successful lesson. You might sometimes be disappointed that a session which began well ended badly. This is often due to a lack of thought about what children will do when their planned task is finished. During your evaluation, consider whether the task was of the correct length for the time you had available. Was it too short, or too long, forcing them to leave things unfinished, or to rush? Consider whether they should have been given more opportunity to use their initiative and develop their own ideas. Would the children have benefitted more from working together, or individually? Could your organisation have been simpler?

Many student teachers plan individual lessons thoroughly but fail to think ahead about continuity and progression – the way future lessons will develop from them. In your evaluations, spend time reflecting on how the child's learning is developing. Consider how your longer-term plans are served by the present session. Begin to look for evidence in the children's work that helps you evaluate their progress. You can gain this evidence in a number of ways:

1. By asking the children to explain to you what they understood, giving them the time and space to do so in a relaxed manner.
2. By comparing their earlier work in the same area with current work, especially in handwriting, presentation, pictures and diagrams.
3. By seeing how well a child has mastered a certain skill, remembering that some skills take a long time to perfect. Manipulating clay, for instance, can be tricky for small hands; wiring a circuit correctly requires both nimble fingers and an understanding of the concept.
4. By totalling the number of correct responses. This is most appropriate in subjects like Mathematics, where exactness is important. On

the other hand, correct answers don't necessarily mean that the child has understood everything.

5. By using a test. Test scores may provide useful additional information to that gained from other evidence.

Finally, don't forget yourself. Do *you* feel satisfied? Are you finding fulfilment in your teaching? Are you keeping a constructive relationship with the class teacher, able to discuss things openly with her? Do you have characteristics which might be hindering your work as a teacher, or enhancing it? Are you using all your ability and skill?

Evaluations should be a valuable part of your planning. Use them effectively, avoid pointless comment and celebrate your successes.

Keeping records

Planning for the future relies to a large extent on knowledge of the past. Teachers base their teaching plans on their pupils' past experiences. They maintain their hold on the past by keeping records.

Record-keeping is becoming more important in schools. You may be asked to maintain the record-sheets that the school uses, though it is more likely that you will be expected to keep your own. (This can be time-consuming and difficult.) Here are some records you could keep:

1. Records that show which areas of the curriculum have been covered and which neglected.

It's important to spend some time on every curriculum area, including ones you feel uncertain about.

2. Records that note concepts and skills which the children appear to have mastered.

Conversation with a child about the Victorian era might demonstrate his understanding of historical time sequences; his ability to manipulate clay successfully may be revealed as he makes a model of an Inca statue; a drawing might show his skills in reproducing detail of the inner structure of a flower; a page of correctly completed Maths can confirm his grasp of the 24-hour clock; reading a paragraph of a reference book fluently can indicate his competence to read and understand non-fiction.

3. Records that show simple progression.

The best example of these is a reading-record which, at bare minimum, shows the names of books selected and read. It is likely that the school will promote a more thorough approach, including space for the child's and/or parent's comment, or a list of particular reading skills, such as an understanding that a text is read from left to right and top to bottom (for beginners) through to the ability to write a summary of a chapter or a book (for proficient readers).

You can spend only a proportion of your time on record-keeping, but it is important to have a clear idea about children's progress if your further planning is to be effective. There are other records which provide evidence of children's progress. For instance, visual records in the classroom through displays of children's work can provide useful and immediate information. In addition to these, the school may have its own tests, especially in reading and Mathematics, to find out how well children are progressing. There are also the compulsory Standard Assessment Tasks, administered to six- to seven-year-olds and ten- to eleven-year-olds once a year. The results are collated and contribute to the reports which schools have to provide for parents.

CHECKPOINTS

1. What records should you keep?
2. Do your records link with your planning?
3. Are you being realistic about the number, length and detail of records you can keep?

Planning and record-keeping lie at the heart of successful teaching. It is important to be systematic and careful. When you have a secure framework, you can afford to be flexible, show initiative and allow for spontaneity. Without this framework, however, your teaching will become a hit-or-miss affair, probably leading to an unsatisfactory conclusion. However, if you take note of the children's progress and adjust your planning accordingly, you will quickly discover an approach that satisfies you, your class teacher, and your expectations for children's learning.

One potential problem with planning is that there is so much to think about at once. This means that some things may have to give way to other, more important, ones. The next chapter shows you how to choose your priorities.

5
CHOICES AND PRIORITIES

The class teacher must have priorities. So many different things compete for her time, some vital, others less important, and one of her most important skills therefore is knowing what to do now, what to do later, and what to leave undone. As you progress through your practice, you will be faced with similar choices. If you can't decide between conflicting priorities, you will be overwhelmed, so use your practice to learn how to be an effective manager of your own time and energy.

Difficult choices

Teachers make hundreds of decisions in the classroom every day. Some of them must be on-the-spot decisions arising from immediate events:

- Do I ignore the child showing off?
- Shall I spend time with the struggling child?
- Should I continue with my introduction to the lesson or send the groups off to work?
- Which child should I select to answer my question?
- When should the class begin tidying up?

'Do I ignore the child showing off?'

60

Others are less immediate but may be just as important. For example:

1. Should I spend break-time in the classroom preparing for the next session, or join the other staff in the staffroom?
2. Shall I put up the wall display after school or help the class teacher with the netball practice?
3. Should I write extensively in my file about the child causing me a headache or photocopy the worksheets for tomorrow morning?
4. Should I meet up with my friends tonight and relax, or mark the children's work?
5. Can I afford to spend time talking with a chatterbox parent before school or should I excuse myself and check that the construction kits are in good order?

What would you choose to do in these cases? To help you decide, keep in mind where your main responsibilities lie. Compare your answers with the following:

1. It is important to talk to staff, and break-time offers a good opportunity. Yet failure to be ready for the next session could quickly lead to a deterioration of your relationship with the children (and therefore the class teacher). Turning up late for a session after break because you were trying to fit a quart into a pint pot over the fifteen minutes is more likely to be interpreted as a lack of judgement than an admirable determination to join in as a member of the staff team.
2. Wall displays and sports practices are both important. However, the appearance of the classroom will affect all the children in the class, netball practice only a few.
3. Writing about troublesome children can be a useful way of relieving your anxiety and considering alternative strategies for dealing with them. On the other hand, it is likely that discussing the issue with the class teacher will be more fruitful. Against this, lack of preparation for the following day can lead to further control problems due to the poor planning and presentation of the lesson.
4. Bleary-eyed students dragging themselves into school at five to nine following a good night out with friends cannot be explained away, however well-earned the night out may have been. Yet the opportunity to speak with other people during the evening about school can help you to understand issues more clearly and put your own problems into perspective.
5. Failure to have the construction kits ready because of a talkative

parent may be seen by the class teacher as poor organisation. On the other hand, the parent may be desperate to talk to you about something serious, so the construction kits may just have to wait.

Setting priorities

All the decisions you must make fall into one of these four categories:

1. NOT URGENT	and	UNIMPORTANT
2. URGENT	but	UNIMPORTANT
3. URGENT	and	IMPORTANT
4. NOT URGENT	but	IMPORTANT

1. Things that are neither urgent nor important should not trouble you at all. Don't waste time on them.
2. Tasks that are urgent but unimportant matter, but only for a while. You can't put them off, but don't waste time worrying about them and trying to be a perfectionist.
3. You have no choice about urgent and important jobs. Do them, *now*! They are emergencies.
4. Tasks in the last category are the most significant. They matter, but because they are not urgent you have time to give them careful thought. For example, planning next week's work for your class is not urgent – yet. It can be started tomorrow evening and you can work on it in detail over the weekend. But it is very important, so plan carefully, to give yourself plenty of time to think about it. Bad planning will mean that the task becomes increasingly urgent, and when things become emergencies they are more likely to get out of your control.

Here are some more situations. Use the categories above to decide how you would react to them:

1. A child working on a computer in the library asks you to stop and explain something as you hurry to the headteacher's room for a meeting. You want to help the child, who is normally shy, but fear being late.
2. Shortly before school begins, you notice that the pencils need sharpening. You need them for your five-year-olds, but want to meet the children at the door as they arrive.

3. As your top juniors are changing for the PE session, the class teacher warns you that the equipment baskets are in a dreadful tangle and will need sorting out. You meant to check them beforehand, but forgot. You're responsible for the class and the hall is on the far side of the school.
4. You were intending to spend some time catching up with your file after school but at the last minute are asked to help out with transport for the girls' netball match at another school. You don't want to appear unhelpful, but are desperate to complete the file.
5. As you cross the playground on the way to the classroom, a child trips and hurts himself badly. You can see that action is needed, but know that it will make you late for your teaching session.
6. You have a dozen paintings to mount and display. You are anxious to put them up as the college tutor urged you to do so during his visit that morning, but you feel exhausted and need to get home early.
7. Another student in the same school has been told by the supervisor that her class teacher is pleased with her progress. As nothing like that was said to you, you feel anxious, and want to speak to the class teacher about it after school. Unfortunately, the person who normally gives you a lift home wants to leave promptly.

These present difficult choices. How would you have reacted? Compare your decisions with the following:

1. Arriving on time for an important meeting with the headteacher must take priority over speaking to a child about their work. The headteacher will expect you to arrive punctually and may see your explanation about the child's need as an excuse. You can arrange to help the child when you have more time.
2. If the pencils are not sharpened and you need them for the next lesson, you should sharpen them quickly. Make sure you check them in advance next time. Meeting children at the door can begin only when you have the practicalities of classroom procedure under control.
3. If your PE lesson depends on the use of small-scale equipment, ensure everything is in order before the session begins. If there's a last-minute hitch, you will have to use the first part of your session as an exercise in sorting the equipment. Don't leave your group unattended while you attempt to do it yourself.

4. Your preparation work and use of your file are priorities. But maintaining good relationships with the staff is equally crucial. In this situation, offer to assist the teacher, but explain your difficulty. The majority of teachers will happily negotiate to give you extra time for working on your file during the following morning. If you can't be sure of the time you need to complete the file, you may have to decline regretfully, but offer to help on another occasion.

5. *The safety of the children takes precedence over everything else.* If children are waiting for you to arrive for a session, don't forget to send another child to the class teacher explaining the circumstances.

6. Display is an important part of your work, but your own well-being is a priority. Go home, rest, and mount the paintings when you feel recovered. The tutor is unlikely to come again for another week, anyway.

7. Insecurity about your progress on the practice can be worrying. It's better to miss your lift and be late home than to spend all night fretting about the problem. Speak to your class teacher at the earliest moment and share your fears.

It's important to be clear about your priorities. You will face many difficult decisions during teaching practice. Some important tasks are urgent and demand immediate action (ensuring the safety of the children and looking after your health, for example). Others are important, but may be less urgent (lesson preparation; maintaining your file; liaising with the class teacher; evaluating your teaching and the children's progress, etc.). Other things will have to take their turn, depending on circumstances. For instance, some headteachers demand high standards of display throughout the school and insist that all staff spend time on it. Other schools have many staff meetings, either as a whole staff or between groups of teachers, to which you may be invited. Still others spend as much time as they can on activities like swimming, looking after an environmental area, or running lunch-time clubs. It is useful if you can help or participate, but be careful not to over-commit yourself.

Remember that the four categories listed earlier are not permanent ones. Important but not urgent things can become important and urgent if you put them off for too long. Sometimes, the urgent and important things, too, can move into another category, for if you put off an urgent decision for too long, you can miss the vital moment and waste the opportunity.

Useful experiences

Some things which happen during teaching practice may not be priorities, but are nevertheless useful experiences in which to involve yourself. For example, taking the register at the start of the morning and afternoon; accompanying the class teacher during playground duty; going with the school team for their match after school. None of these may be central to the task of learning how to teach, but all are very useful in learning how to be a teacher. Take every opportunity to gain experience and show a willingness to get involved, as long as it does not push other, more important priorities, off your list. You will find yourself running out of energy if you take on too many commitments, but later on, when you are confident that your major priorities are under control, you may feel able to cope with extras like these.

Safeguarding children

Whatever the activity you choose to do with your class, the highest priority of all must be that it is *safe*. Sometimes the extent of risk to the children leaves no room for choice: the activity is unacceptable.

Children's welfare is so important that it should always influence your choice of activities. But how far? Should the teacher never take risks, always play safe, and in doing so risk denying the children learning opportunities which might benefit them? Listed below are a number of situations where a student teacher's ambition may be tempered by a concern about the well-being of the children and others. Each one involves a small element of risk. Where should your priorities lie?

1. In Science and Technology you want to make self-propelled wheeled vehicles that can negotiate uneven surfaces. You discuss provisional ideas with the children and realise that their plans will require the use of sharp tools and a hot glue-gun. You are anxious to develop these ideas but hesitate because of the dangers.

Much depends upon the age of the children and their previous experience so it pays to check with the class teacher about the suitability of the equipment. Many teachers have experience of injuries to children using sharp and hot equipment, so you are right to be cautious. However, if the children have been properly trained, and if you can spend time with those handling the equipment, use whatever is available. Watch out for the child who uses equipment for the wrong purpose, even (on occasions) as weapons for harming another pupil. Restrict the use of equipment to the trained group.

2. You want to move furniture about to allow for greater collaboration in an exercise using local maps but fear that it might prove too disruptive and interfere with movement about the room.

If you are working with large sheets, you will obviously need more space than usual. You may be in a position where you can take the children out of the classroom and into a less busy area to work. This is fine if you are responsible for only a single group, but if there are other children in the classroom for whom you are responsible, you will need to bear in mind the practicalities of moving to and fro. Movement of furniture can open up possibilities for imaginative approaches, including larger numbers of children working together on large-scale joint enterprises. You may want to create a one-way system of movement around the room to avoid squashing. Don't hesitate to move furniture if it will create the right conditions for improved teaching and learning, but don't forget to reorganise afterwards. In the unlikely need to evacuate the room quickly, exit points must be clear of possible obstructions, like tables. Make a habit of checking that bags are not blocking gangways. There will be a fire regulations sheet somewhere in the room; check that you know the routine.

3. You want to extend your infants' experience with sand and water and have developed some exciting activities which may cause a mess. You are uncertain whether your plan is practical in your small classroom.

It is likely that part of the floor is carpeted and can't be used for sand and water activities. Bear in mind the extra space needed. If you use any corridor space, take care to keep walkways clear, and avoid doorways and entrance points. Remember that the children themselves need protection. Small but important points, such as ensuring that sleeves are rolled up and encouraging young children to tie one another's aprons, can add to the value of the exercise.

4. You want to use apparatus in the hall. You're conscious that accidents are more likely there than in any other setting, but you don't want to deny the children or yourself the use of the apparatus.

You are right in thinking that the hall can be a dangerous place. It is essential to check equipment before the lesson and ensure that you are familiar with its use. The class teacher will normally stay with you during the lesson. If the children don't have the correct footwear, consider allowing them to do PE in bare feet. Never permit them to wear only socks, for fear of skids and slips. If the children are barefooted, seek advice about moving apparatus. (Construction workers on a building site wear steel-capped shoes as protection against heavy items damaging their feet; children using large equipment are no less vulnerable.)

The principles of safety and order are true for other hall activities. Young children love to whoop about, and older ones often delight in near misses. It's usually the innocent who get hurt, so decide how much free activity of this kind is necessary. Also, *check what you should do if there is an incident requiring medical assistance.*

Some activities require a lot of organisation and firm control of the class. Whereas a difficult session can be avoided by playing safe and choosing something less demanding, there is everything to be gained from exciting, innovative lessons, especially if you have sought advice from the class teacher beforehand and explained your problem. Providing you are clear about your intentions and organisation, creative activities that allow for individual initiative and spontaneity can result in satisfying whole-class work that leads to unity of purpose and harmony. There is often a small risk associated with interesting activities, so you should take precautions to protect the children from harm. But if your teaching is to rise above the ordinary, you must be bold.

'There is often a small risk associated with interesting activities.'

Choices that demand extra effort

Other choices in the classroom will test your own and the class teacher's priorities. They don't carry the risks described above, but they do demand your time, energy, and expertise and therefore present further choices about your options.

As you move through your teaching practice, you will gradually feel more at home in the classroom, and reach the point where you refer to the room as 'yours'. Your early struggles to settle in will be replaced by an urge to express in public your own teaching skills and flair. One obvious way is through the appearance of the room. Have you given sufficient thought and time to making it an attractive learning environment? What impression would a visitor receive?

The construction of a large collage or model can take up a lot of space and many hours of time which you might have used for other important tasks. You will have to weigh up whether the effort is justified. One student teacher worked with a group of five children to produce a magnificent mural of a local saint for an exhibition in the local parish church, but paid far too little attention to other aspects of planning and lesson presentation, which led to an imbalance of quality in her teaching. Another student (at the same stage in his course), working with infants, managed to produce an exciting range of activities which led to a wonderful display of puppets with moving parts, without neglecting the other areas of the practice. A third student used a huge scrambling net in the centre of the room as a focal point for display arising from her project, again without losing track of the need to pay attention to other aspects of her work.

Finally, remember that the appearance of classrooms matters to schools, especially to the headteacher showing prospective parents around. Interesting displays suggest that the teachers are well organised, value children's work, and want to use resources efficiently. The efforts that you make will be noticed and appreciated by the children and class teacher.

Opportunities beyond the classroom

The teacher's role extends beyond the classroom door. There are many activities and duties with which a teacher must engage and it's a good idea to spend some time familiarising yourself with some of them. They will give you fresh insight into the fuller role of the teacher. As you consider the following range of activities, consider how you might fit them into your busy schedule. What can you learn from them about:

- A teacher's responsibilities?
- Children's attitude and behaviour?
- The headteacher's expectations?
- Thorough organisation?
- Liaison with parents?

Playground duty

Each school has a rota of staff responsible for patrolling the playground. In some schools this may involve more than one teacher. If possible, go out on patrol with your own class teacher once or twice to get an insight into this demanding task. Watch how she arbitrates between children's conflicting claims during a squabble. Notice how she prevents possible accidents and deals with them when they happen. Observe the routine for children entering school at the end of playtime.

You will find playground duty exciting and exhausting. Exciting because, when you first walk into a playground as the adult in charge,* you realise what a responsibility you have, surrounded by large numbers of children. Exhausting because infant children often want to hold

---

* Make sure you are accompanied by another teacher, for it is illegal to be alone on duty until you are fully qualified.

your hand or chase excitedly around you. Juniors may ask you for permission to do something they know the class teacher would refuse (so always refer them to her). Children are ever moving, and you seem to need eyes everywhere.

Playground duty gives you the opportunity to watch children without the need to teach them. Watch how their behaviour differs from that in the classroom. Watch the patterns of interaction to see who is friends with whom (and who are enemies). Notice the broad groupings into boys and girls and look for the exceptions, especially towards the top of the junior phase. Notice the range of games played, and think about the inventiveness of many children. See which children are assertive and boisterous and which are timid and peaceable. The insights you gain can prove useful in the teaching situation and may alert you to relationship issues, or cause you to rethink your view of a child's character and potential.

Faced with so many priorities, you may feel that doing playground duty may be adding one too many. But the insights you will gain from watching children outside the classroom environment could be of such value that you will want to put it close to the top of your list.

Assembly

Schools are obliged to hold an act of worship each day for every child.*
Some people think of assembly as a hollow ritual, others as a period of great importance in the day, when all members of the school can come together in one community, helping to shape and promote the school's identity. If you have the opportunity to be involved in an assembly led by your class, take it. Your support and contribution will be important to the class teacher and to the children. (Attend only when you are certain that you are ready for the rest of the day ahead.) If you have any talents to offer, such as the ability to play an instrument, or skills in dance and drama, you will find that most teachers will welcome your assistance. Remember that the class assembly is a public occasion, when other teachers and perhaps the headteacher and parents will watch your class teacher at work with her class.

---

* Schools sometimes hold separate assemblies for different religious groups because their parents would object on religious grounds to attendance at the main assembly. Those children are normally kept apart in a classroom, supervised by a teacher.

All assemblies can teach you something:

- They give you the chance to see professionals at work.
- They can let you see a cross-section of the local community.
- They help you to gauge the true purpose of assemblies.

Contact with parents

Parents have always been important to the life and well-being of the school, so take the opportunity to meet them and show enthusiasm for what their child has done and what qualities he or she possesses. There are a number of places to meet parents:

1. The best time is when they bring their child into the building at the start of the day or collect them at the end of school.
2. Sometimes parents will come in for a special purpose such as an assembly, as a helper on a school trip or for an open day, when they are encouraged to come into school to look around and talk to the teachers.
3. Other parents spend time regularly in school as unpaid classroom assistants; perhaps to mend books, help a group with cooking, or hear children read.
4. Some parents are members of the governing body and so belong in the school not only as clients but as people responsible for what goes on there.

Parents can teach you a lot about school life. Listen to their comments; take note of their questions; find out what matters to them. Parents see and hear a lot around the school, sometimes having a degree of access denied even to teachers. They will often be a source of encouragement, helping you to keep things in perspective by their down-to-earth comments. However, be careful not to discuss confidential issues with them (except, of course, concerning their own child) or talk to them at the expense of time spent with the class teacher.

There are many choices facing you as you proceed through teaching practice. Sometimes you will choose badly, but this is part of your learning process, so don't let one or two mistakes cause you to become timid. Properly ordered priorities, both inside and outside the classroom, should enhance your practice – both for you and for those you teach.

6

LOOKING BACK, LOOKING FORWARD

As you come to the end of your teaching practice and reflect upon your time in school, you will want to ask yourself how much you have achieved and how much there remains to achieve. Further periods in school may lie ahead during your course, and it is essential that you use the intervening time well. It will help to review your progress under three headings:

1. Planning, teaching and assessment
2. Relationships with the children
3. Relationships with the staff

You will have had your tutor's and class-teacher's comments throughout the practice, and a final report, to assist you in your evaluation.

1. Planning, teaching and assessment

Reread the lesson aims and evaluations in your file:

- Were those aims fulfilled?
- Was your organisation adequately thought through?
- Is there evidence that the children learned anything?

By now you should have had experience of handling a variety of teaching situations. You will know that sometimes things worked out as expected and sometimes that they didn't.

- How often was the outcome the result of good (or poor) planning?
- How do you know?

Perhaps you planned the lesson so carefully that you failed to allow any space for spontaneity or for using the children's ideas. New teachers can become obsessed with planning and fail to be flexible enough. If you reached the stage in your practice where you planned carefully, but were able to put your plans to one side during the lesson and concentrate on interacting with your pupils, you probably achieved a good balance between prior planning and spontaneity.

Failures

Look back at a lesson for which you thought you had prepared thoroughly but in which the results were disappointing. Perhaps:

1. The children seemed uninterested, or
2. The quality of work they produced was indifferent.

1. If the children were uninterested, perhaps:

- Your early presentation was uninspiring and the children assumed that the content of the lesson would be similarly tedious.
- The work seemed irrelevant to them.
- The task was too easy (they weren't stretched enough) or too difficult (they didn't have the understanding and knowledge required).
- They were in the wrong frame of mind owing to circumstances beyond your control.
- You put the children in the wrong frame of mind by your attitude (misjudging the mood and being too soft or too harsh, for example).

These are all learning points which can guide improvement.

'They were in the wrong frame of mind due to circumstances beyond your control.'

73

- Did you get excited about the content yourself and communicate your enthusiasm to the children?
- Did you capture their interest or imagination?
- Did you assume that because you had spent ages in preparing the lesson, the children would automatically find it fascinating?

When you repeat this lesson with another class, spend more time linking the work with their previous experience. Explain where it's leading. Convince them by your enthusiasm that it's an important thing for them to be doing.

- Did you use inappropriate vocabulary and fail to give the children time to ask questions?
- Did you move too quickly through the lesson, giving insufficient time for them to digest its content?

Next time, check their understanding more regularly during the lesson.

2. If the quality of the work was poor, consider whether you were in any way responsible:

- Did you follow an interesting introduction or practical activity with a dull instruction? (Perhaps this led to chimes of 'Do we have to?' from the children.)
- Did you fail to make your intentions clear, resulting in a casual approach by the children to what you hoped would be a polished piece of work?
- Did you give the children insufficient time to complete their work? Did this lead to rushed work of low quality?
- Did the children think that because you were not their class teacher, you didn't have to be treated seriously? Did you reinforce this view by allowing shoddy work or low standards to pass unremarked?
- Did you give opportunities for more able children to extend their learning while making allowances for slower ones?
- Were your expectations of the children's ability high enough?

Successes

Now look back at times when your lesson succeeded, either because it was an unexpected triumph, or (more probably) because it seemed to meet your expectations. What characterised those times? It may be difficult to pin down exactly why a lesson was a success, but here are some possibilities:

- You had gone to a lot of trouble to plan carefully and match the task to the children's ability.
- You were knowledgeable about the lesson's content.
- You enjoyed a good relationship with the children, having earned their trust and respect, and were firm in your handling of the situation and positive in your attitude.
- You enjoyed what you were teaching and this transmitted itself to the children.
- You paced the lesson well, introduced it in an imaginative way, and allowed sufficient time both for the task and clearing away.
- You had discussed the lesson beforehand with the class teacher and carefully considered her advice.
- You had seen someone else carry out a similar lesson and learned from their experience.

Perhaps a lesson went well when there was no obvious reason for it to be successful. Consider whether this was one of those occasions when you were able to forget your detailed planning and just enjoy the freedom and excitement of learning. Such experiences are the essence of good teaching, so cherish them.

Your teaching will improve as you learn to make *assessment* an integral factor in planning lessons. If you have seen it only as an extra chore, divorced from the main lesson, you will have lost sight of its purpose, which is to act as a guide to more effective teaching. On the other hand, if you used assessment as a method of continually monitoring progress, and modified your lessons accordingly, you will have taken an important step forward.

2. Relationships with the children

You will have discovered throughout the practice that merely liking children is not enough to make someone a good teacher, yet the relationships you had with the children were highly significant. As you reflect upon your time in school, certain children will remain etched into your memory and others will quickly fade. What causes

'Certain children will remain etched into your memory.'

this? Why did some children leap forward under your influence while others stood still – or even seemed to move backwards?

This book should have convinced you that respect and fairness towards all pupils is essential. As a principled teacher, you will have tried to ensure that you did not show unreasonable preference to any particular child. On the other hand, you will have realised that not all children require the same degree of time and attention. Slower learners and insecure children often need extra help with their work. The danger of spending too much time with any one group is clear; some teachers unwittingly spend a great deal of time with bright children and so put little effort into assisting the more passive ones.

The quality of the time spent has also influenced your relationships and how well the children learned. A few moments' intervention with a child who is struggling, giving clear, concise guidance at the appropriate time, should have had positive results. By contrast, some children may have become too dependent upon you, so that time spent with them was of no benefit. You realised that they needed to become more independent in their work, or perhaps learn to work collaboratively with other children, rather than rely too much on you. In the light of these factors:

- Did you spend more time with certain groups or individuals than was necessary?
- Did you respond to some children with less enthusiasm and interest than to others?
- Have you damaged a child's self-esteem by undervaluing their efforts?

These can be painful questions for a teacher to ask. Next time you teach, try to monitor your attitude to different children by being more aware of your responses and comments.

Developing a good relationship with children will necessitate taking account of who they are and what is important to them. Children with different backgrounds from those of the majority need to feel that you value them and their cultural identity. If you have failed to give adequate recognition to the diversity of cultures, backgrounds and beliefs existing within your class, you have missed a learning opportunity and may have unintentionally made some children feel less valued.

Where do you see the links between establishing good relationships between teacher and taught, and the quality of the teaching and learning? During your preliminary visit, prior to the practice, it was almost certainly the children who made the biggest impression on you. Now, as your practice draws to a close, the same is probably still true.

There will be some children who are sorry to see you leave. It is not sentimental of you to acknowledge that your relationship with those children has contributed towards their welfare, confidence and desire to learn. Your efforts and hard work have not been in vain.

CHECKPOINTS

When you next teach a group of children:

1. How will you establish acceptable standards of behaviour to ensure that they have the best atmosphere in which to learn?
2. How will you convince the children that you are to be trusted?
3. How will you give the children appropriate amounts of your time and effort?
4. How will you allow for the children's differing personalities and backgrounds?

3. Relationships with the staff

You will have discovered that many of your colleagues in the school, especially the class teacher, have played an important part in guiding you through the practice. Your enthusiasm, willingness to try ideas, and openness should have convinced your class teacher that you are someone to be trusted with the teaching of her children. Put yourself in the place of the teachers in the school. What did they expect from you? After qualifying, you will have new teachers of your own to work with. What will you expect from them?

There are many opportunities during school practice to make a good impression on other staff. Paying attention to timekeeping, keeping people informed, showing a willingness to learn from others, being ready to contribute – all are a necessary part of developing as a professional. And don't overlook the importance of using the staffroom regularly and assisting in the upkeep of its appearance.

Putting things in perspective

If you didn't make any mistakes during your teaching practice, please write and inform the author to receive your gold-plated stick of chalk! To make the best of your time in school, you will have learned from your mistakes rather than dwelling on them, and realised that even seasoned professionals stumble from time to time. In fact, you will have believed your class teacher when she told you that the longer she taught, the more there seemed to be to learn about the job. You were therefore honest about your failings, but avoided being unnecessarily gloomy. You impressed others by tackling difficulties directly, asking advice, staying cheerful and putting things in perspective.

On the other hand, you were also able to enjoy the successes. You didn't allow one good lesson to convince you that you'd 'made it', but you rightly felt elated that your hard work paid off. You learned to revel in the joys of teaching as well as keeping failures in proportion.

What have you learned?

Above all, the teaching practice will have taught you a lot about yourself. You will have channelled all your energies into classroom work, keeping control, anxious that the children increase their knowledge, developing their understanding, practising skills, and having the opportunity to work creatively. They will have benefitted from all your efforts – but you, too, will have been influenced by the practice. As you reflect upon your time spent in school, consider how you have changed and progressed.

You have gained in confidence. You now know that you can cope with the considerable demands of teaching practice. You have responded to what was asked of you, and succeeded – even prospered. Your first few days in school now seem like another lifetime. This doesn't mean, of course, that everything will be smooth and easy from now on. You are aware that the challenges which face every teacher will be there again next time, when you are in a different school, with a different class.

You will have a better understanding of the curriculum. As you have looked at the National Curriculum documents and tried to present ideas in an interesting, appropriate manner, you have learned a lot about those things too. You may even be able to speak now with some authority about things that were formerly unclear. The act of teaching carries with it a responsibility to be well-informed about subject content, and you will have progressed in this.

You will have gained important *skills* during the practice, both in teaching areas of the curriculum and in handling children. But above all, you are nearer to becoming a professional. Although you will probably be sorry to leave the teaching-practice school, and may find saying goodbye to the children an emotional wrench, it is true to say that within a very short time you will be forgotten by most staff and pupils. So it's important to remind yourself that *you* are the one constant factor in your teaching career. As you consider what you did on your teaching practice, how you felt, and what you understood, remember that your thinking, feeling, and understanding about educational issues must continue. Although the class you're leaving behind may not play any further role in your life, there are many other children yet to meet you, influence you, and be influenced by you.

Finally, remember that schools are imperfect places. But by constantly striving to develop an informed view of what education is all about, you can use your personal qualities, clarity of purpose, knowledge, and whole-hearted commitment to become the high-quality professional the children in our schools deserve.

FURTHER READING

Bassey, M. (1989), *Teaching Practice in the Primary School* (London: Ward Lock Educational)

Cortazzi, M. (1991), *Primary Teaching: How It Is* (London: Fulton)

Dean, J. (2nd edition, 1991), *Organising Learning in the Primary School Classroom* (London: Routledge)

Kyriacou, C. (1986), *Effective Teaching in Schools* (Oxford: Blackwell)

Pinder, R. (1987), *Why Don't Teachers Teach Like They Used To?* (London: Hilary Shipman)

Pollard, A. (1985), *The Social World of the Primary School* (London: Cassell)